ΓH THANKS

Some of the characters who play a part in Max, the situations in which they find themselves and the things they say, owe something to real people and therefore I thank the following who provided some elements of inspiration as I pieced this story together. Some are also acknowledged in the names of the characters who may or may not bear some resemblance to their namesakes.

Tom Anderson, Flo Bairstow, Janice Denyer, Mel Gibson, David Jago, Frankie Lane and Vivian Stanshall

And to my team of readers, who tried their best to keep up with the plot, for their provision of valuable feedback during the process of writing

Alice Roscoe, Barry Mitchinson, Eric Hartley, Gloria Deacon, Steve Phillip, Sharon Roscoe and Judith Sharod

MAX

A story for those who want to lead
others to excellence

MAX

LEARNING TO LEAD: OK IS A START, EXCELLENCE AN AMBITION

A sideways look for managers at the fundamentals of: goal setting and action planning, managing performance, leading change and the significance of a desire for personal development

GORDON ROSCOE

Matador
5 Weir Road
Kibworth Beauchamp
Leicester LE8 0LQ, UK
Tel: 0116 279 2277
Email: books@troubador.co.uk
Web: www.troubador.co.uk/matador

ISBN 978 1848764 286

British Library Cataloguing in Publication Data.
A catalogue record for this book is available from the British Library.

Illustrations: Rob Anderson

Printed in the UK by TJ International, Padstow, Cornwall

Matador Business is an imprint of Troubador Publishing Ltd

CONTENTS

WHAT'S GOING ON HERE?

Developing ourselves as managers and leaders is a challenge; to do it we must deal with some important though tedious information. Well at least that's my view. It helps if learning is fun ... but sometimes that is easier said than done.

Max is a story about leadership skills for managers. The advice it offers is tried and tested but, for me, reading this stuff presented sensibly and logically in a text book is devastatingly dull. To those for whom that approach works, I mean not to offend, but if that is you this may be the moment to pass MAX on to a colleague.

For those who are still with me, I have chosen to weave what I believe are important learning points into an adventure story. I have chosen to cover subjects which, when added to those covered by HIDDEN TREASURE, will equip any manager to significantly improve the impact of their leadership. In my view, the most important omission to these ideas is the work of R. Meredith Belbin on team roles, and I would advise the dedicated self-developer to become familiar with this.

The structure of MAX is intended to help by both keeping you interested and presenting important ideas in a context that should assist you to understand their implications and how they can be applied. All subject chapters have both a set of learning questions at the end and a learning summary. If you take the time to answer the learning questions it will help you both understand and remember. The learning summary is a factual summing up of the core learning points, and given that repetition is the mother of learning, I hope that this short finish to each chapter will help bring ideas together for you.

1
MAX

Imagine a simple measuring scale: it has on it only three points of calibration; Poor, OK and Excellent. Poor is far less than could have been achieved; it is a result with which we must be disappointed. OK is something neither Poor nor Excellent; it is passable, acceptable but not remarkable. Excellent is something that is in the higher range of our potential; it is much more than OK, it is something to be proud of and worthy of positive comment and praise.

There are many things to which we can apply our scale: How did I do at school? How well did I repair that broken fence? How did I manage that confrontation? Our use of the scale is personal; it depends upon our outlook, expectations and standards. One person may feel that at school they achieved excellence because they succeeded at sport, made many lifelong friends and left at 16 well prepared to begin work. Another having this experience but focussed on the achievement of qualifications would feel that they had failed, and therefore on our scale their performance was Poor. Notice that I am asking you to apply this measure to yourself, to your behaviour and activities. This is personal.

We are about to take a journey together, one that

is focussed on achievement and one on which you will constantly be asked to consider the question, 'How well am I doing?' If you have read my first book "HIDDEN TREASURE" you will have considered the skills needed as a manager and leader of others, to get people to work together as a team. HIDDEN TREASUE encourages leaders to see people as potential and describes the leadership skills needed to begin to uncover that potential. Assertive Communication, Leadership, Coaching, Delegation and Team Building are considered, along with how these things inter-relate. By applying this knowledge you should safely move your managerial performance to OK. This may seem lacking in ambition but, as a start, the achievement of OK is a significant step forward, it is the difference between survival and failure, between a career where you sustain yourself and your family or one distinguished by frustration and failure.

You are about to meet Max. Max is you, your potential and friend. Max is here to take you a step further towards excellence. Max asks questions about leadership. How is it that some teams perform better than others? What distinguishes those that do ok from those that excel? What marks out the competent from outstanding performer? Max will challenge you to do better than OK.

Max has a second objective with regard to your imagination; it is to set it to work and to use it effectively in developing yourself. If you are of an imaginative disposition then this will be no challenge; if you are someone who thinks that other people have all the ideas and that the world is better grounded in reality than flights of fancy, then you may have more work to do here. Without imagination you cannot progress; if you cannot imagine a better time or better self, if you cannot imagine the finished outcome of an activity, then you will struggle to reach your goal. We all use our imagination constantly: we usually get into a car, bus or train with our destination in mind (imagination), a bricklayer lays the first brick with the finished result in mind (imagination), a doctor asks questions of a sick patient with many possibilities in mind, the answer to each question narrowing those possibilities (imagination). To imagine is to use our mind to see something that we cannot see with our eyes. Some of us are told, when young, that we have no imagination and, because we are young and absorb ideas readily, we believe the message, hampering greatly our ability to move forward in life. If that is you, then challenge that belief. It is false. Who told you this? When did you come to believe it? Has the belief helped or hindered you? Is it time to put that belief aside and believe something else?

To be successful at anything you must exercise your imagination, and the more you use it the better you become at using it. Max will ask you to imagine many things that you cannot see. I urge you to use your mind to add detail to the scenes described, to imagine with your senses what the characters feel, see, hear, smell and taste. The better you get at doing this, the better you become at imagining your own future and the better able you are to achieve success.

Now it is time. Flex that imagination, determine to seek excellence, turn the page and …

37
OVER THE TOP

A pebble, caught by the toe of my boot, leaps like a determined lemming over the edge into empty air. I watch it disappearing downward, falling. I breathe in hard, step onto that same edge, look up into the sky and jump.

I had thought about how the drop might be. If it were feet first what would you see as you fell? If you hit the ground in that position would the result look worse than headfirst? Why should I care? But I found that I did. Perhaps you would splay out as you fell, skydiver style, riding the thermals; surely more graceful and surely a more impressive splat, or would that be crunch?

Somehow I have made a dive. I am flying superhero style (I should have worn a cape), arms stretched forward, fingertips meeting, together pointing, toward the ground. I am an arrow. I feel air rushing past me, although I suppose I am rushing past it. 'It' pushes into my eyes, drags my hair back, fills my sleeves into shuddering rolls. I am surprised. I thought (and how I have thought about this for weeks before today) that this would be quick – short, sharp and over. But it is the opposite. My senses seem to stretch time, giving me room to think, and the thoughts that come are predictable.

Are my thoughts of childhood, school, family, love life? No, I think about the source of my stress, of how I first became a manager. I was 23 and given a supervisory role over two guys my own age. We worked well together and the role was easily fulfilled. In truth we just got on with our work and I reported to our boss; but I had the glorious title of 'manager'. I had made it!

We did well and I was promoted to manage a different department, and that's when things got tricky. What was I supposed to do when they didn't do what I asked of them or when they didn't do things how I wanted them done? Some of them couldn't take criticism without sulking for the rest of the day, and some seemed to resent me (I think they were the ones who wanted the manager's job that I got). My solution was to work harder and try to keep everyone happy. I remembered that my own boss shouted at people when they got things wrong, so I did the same. After all, I didn't want to lose control did I? Things didn't go well and thank goodness I had the fortune to stumble across some leadership training and came to understand the concept of Hidden Treasure, which is to recognise the potential within people and how to get to it by leading them to work together as a team. I realised how managers can get people to perform, how people perform best when they are in teams and what skills are needed to create a team (Assertive Communication, Leadership, Coaching, Delegation, Motivation and Team Building). I steadily built my skill at team building and gained a reputation for developing my people and getting results.

But as the years passed I recognised a problem that has come to haunt me, which has made my working life a disappointment. The problem is this: while I succeed in getting people to work together I always seem to find myself in second place. My teams do well and I am recognised as a safe pair of hands – but I don't excel. Others get there before me; show the stroke of genius that lands the big prize. Now look at me: 37 years of age, heading toward the big 4 – O, all my life I have thought that one day I would be a real achiever, and now it seems I must settle for being average. That really hurts. Destined to succeed but never excel – that is not how I see myself. And it bugs me, especially when I see my friends doing well, doing so much better than me. There's just one question I would love to answer: 'Why can't I get my team members to perform to the MAAAAAAAX?'

My stomach and nose seem to collide, my eyes snap wide open and I see the ground before me – receding! Ohh noooooooooo; I'm going UP not down! Oh here we go now, its DOWN not up. My ears regain their ability to hear, and I hear shouts, 'BUNGEEEEEE'. It's the gang shouting at me and laughing; looks like I survived my one and only bungee jump. I raised the money, but never again!

Back on the ground I join the others who had each jumped before me. They claim I looked the most scared on the way down. Big smiles all round, comrades in bungee, united by our ordeal. We were the famous five, well that's what we called ourselves when we shared together back in our 20's, when life was uncomplicated and each of us bursting with potential. There's Mel, who looks like a bronzed god, never ceases to attract the ladies and has always failed to be able to explain to me how to do it; Flo, who makes the guys look like sissies and is my best mate; Tom, who must have the biggest brain in the universe, and we all love him because he's so off-beat and Janice, who is graceful and gifted and makes you feel the same (well within your physical limitations, you understand). And now we're off to the pub, as we have been so many times before, but this time as full blooded brothers and sisters in bungee. 'See you down there,' I say walking off to find the car, fumbling in my pocket for the keys.

'Howdee,' drawls a deep dark voice. I leap, really high, still wound up from the jump. This voice is right by my ear. I look round, nothing; behind me, next to me; nothing. 'Howdee pardner – long time no see.' The voice is so deep and rich you could wade through it and still it's somehow right in my ear.

'Who the …' I am spinning round trying to find the speaker and then I spot a figure 20 yards away. A figure on a horse that is somehow familiar. The man and horse are beneath a tree and I sense that they are the source of the voice.

'You gonna talk to me old bud?'

'Who the hell are you, is that you over there?' I am confused thinking *am I in shock, hallucinating?*

'You forgotten your old buddy?' Perhaps familiar, the voice is still close, but now I can see that the man on the horse is its owner, he is looking at me and moving his mouth as I hear the words. The horse looks at me too. I walk towards him and as I get closer I see he is a cowboy, right out of the Wild West: Stetson hat, chaps, leather boots, spurs, six guns. I think I need a drink, or maybe I've had one. What is happening? The figure seems familiar, but from where?

'Buddy come on, we were such good friends. You forgotten old Max?'

WHAM, slam – oh my crikey aunt. Max. It's Max! But Max doesn't, didn't exist. Max was just…

'You know how long it's been buddy?'

'No Max,' *hell now I'm talking to him. HE'S NOT REAL!!*

'29 years buddy, 29 years. You were just 8 that night you said "so long".'

'Max this isn't real.' *Stop talking, I'm losing the plot here.*

'What's your point buddy, I'm your imaginary friend yeah? Just like I always was, yeah?'

My jaw must be round my ankles as I manage a 'yeah' in return.

'You tell me you'll call me when you need me and you don't call for 29 years. That might offend some guys but not your old pal Max, see I like you buddy. Or at least I did 29 years ago, guess you might have changed a bit hey?'

'Max you don't exist.'

'Oh my you have changed. That never used to bother you. Got a problem with imaginary friends now?'

'No, well yes as a matter of fact I think I have. You don't exist.'

'Your conversation has gone downhill, buddy, you used to say more than "you don't exist". Max's voice lowered a few tones and he leaned down toward me 'Hey, remember when you saved me from dying of thirst out in the desert with them coyotes waiting to chew our bones, or when we fought our way out of that corral back to back? You never left me buddy, kept firing, saved my skin. I owe you. Max never forgets a buddy'.

'Max I…..' I really couldn't find any words so Max kept going.

'You used to tell me stories; make up games; we used to have adventures. Fact I was hoping we could have some more since you called for me.'

'I didn't call for you.' The words burst out of my spinning head.

'Why you shouting at Max, buddy?'

'I'm not your buddy. Stop this. Just go away Max, someone might see you.'

'Think you've forgotten something buddy; no one can see me except you, always was and still is. I'm in your imagination, no one else's.'

'But I didn't call you, I'd forgotten all about you, for goodness sake.' Max goes quiet. As he turns his face away I see a hurt look in his eyes.

'Hey Max no offence but I'm 37, I mean you just don't have imaginary friends when you're a grown up'.

'Oh no, then who am I?' the dark drawl is tinged with some impatience now. 'You call me back, call for help and then pretend you don't know me. Me your old buddy who was inseparable, who adventured with you everywhere.'

'I didn't call for help Max.'

'Oh no, then what does screaming MAAAAAAAX mean with your lungs inside out and the fear of death in your nose? A fine old friend you're turning out to be, dragging me from deep just to insult your old buddy.'

'Max I don't mean to insult you but how could you help me?'

'You must have lost your imagination somewhere in those last 29 years; don't you remember that old Max can take you anywhere and find out anything?'

'Yes I do now you remind me, but you are after all just a part of my imagination.'

'JUST!' Max seems to be getting warmed up and his deep voice is booming. I look round, but the few people that are in sight seem oblivious to us. 'Just your imagination – listen here buddy, I can still go anywhere and find out anything. You called me back good and proper, and when you did that you also showed old Max just what's eatin' you. Now you gonna come with me and find out the answers?'

'What?'

'Oh jimminy buddy, you gonna be just as dumb for another 29 years or you gonna come along?'

'Come along how?' Now I'm looking round again: a couple pass hand in hand: 'Outrageous darling,' he says. 'Yes dear, sorry dear,' she replies. A mother playing with some young kids; a man walking a dog; no one's looking at me, no one's interested in me talking to an imaginary cowboy and contemplating getting on the back of his imaginary horse. The horse neighs and paws the ground.

'Come on buddy, Excellence is getting impatient. We got places to go, sights to see, problems to solve'. I'll swear the horse winks at me as I step up to Max and raise my hand. He reaches down and grabs me firmly. He feels real and I lift my foot into the offered stirrup and, whoah, he pulls and I'm up behind him! As I hit the saddle there's a wumph. By that I mean a soft fluffy sound around me, which leaves a muffled effect on the sights and sounds of the field that I just stepped up from. ' Now they can't see yah buddy, just like old times.. Git'… and with that he spurs Excellence, who throws back his fabulous head and begins to gallop, or is it fly or glide? We appear to be galloping into a grey fog.

'Hold tight buddy we gonna solve ya problems. Yeeee ha'.

THE RODEO AND THE IMPOSSIBLE (GOALS AND ACTIONS)

Part 1

Grey fog; green light; white light; buildings; a road; people, 'Hey Max where are we?'

I am conscious of the movement of the horse and we are cantering along a familiar road. I know where we are, I used to work along here. Now we are riding to a building, and as we do I notice some old stuff around, out of date cars and an odd look to the few people we pass. More curious is the way no one takes any notice of us: a cowboy, a horse and bewildered staring me!

We approach the building and Max is riding us straight towards the wall. My senses try to keep up and fail; I close my eyes in confusion and wait for a collision that does not come. I open one eye and we appear to be passing through walls. Then we are inside, but I don't know how we got here. Max has stopped Ex in the doorway of an office that I know so well. What I see, as I lean around Max who sits astride the horse in front of me, causes me to gape, speechless; again!

It's me. It can't be. It is, a much younger me. I am sitting behind the desk that I used to sit behind. The sun is streaming through the window and three others are with me in a meeting.

'Max. Explain,' I whisper.

'No need to whisper, bud, they can't hear you.'

'That's me, isn't it?'

' Yes, we just went back 14 years; that's you alright.'

' Max help me. What's happened here?'

'We've gone back, old friend. We've gone back to see where you went wrong. Remember this?'

'Yes, that's the three J's.'

'You kiddin' me, old bud?'

'No they were called James, John and Jeanne, so I called 'em the three J's: Jimmy, Johnny and Jeanne.'

'And you're saying my world is strange?'

'Yes, but how are we …?' I run out of words again, because I have started talking. I mean that me over there, 14 years younger, has started talking. I can do no more than watch and listen and give up thinking about what is happening before my brain implodes.

'We've got three weeks to do this, three weeks to hit this target. We need to work together and work smart. Do I have your support?' Nods from the trio.

'I want your ideas, I want you involved in the planning. How do you feel about that?'

'Yes great,' says Jeanne, and she begins to suggest ideas while the others chip in with their own thoughts. Then it's Johnnie who takes up the talk, sounds like Jeanne inspired him. The group of four, that includes me, are animated and excited as the ideas flow. Jimmy is quieter but makes notes.

I remember this meeting, I felt like I was effectively leading my team. I had them motivated, wanting to make it work. I had done all the right things, involved them, inspired and motivated them, delegated key tasks so that they were developing and learning new things as we went along. I had a team, a real motivated team, all looking out for each other and committed to working hard towards a common cause. How could we go wrong? By the end of the meeting all four of us had agreed to put in place new ideas for boosting sales; we would each go away from the meeting and work hard. And we did, I'm certain we did. I watched the meeting finish and the three J's left the room. I watched myself pick up the phone and call my boss to tell him that I was confident that my team and I would rise to the challenge.

Woaaah! Ex reared up on his hind legs and I gripped Max's shoulders to stay on the horse. Ex didn't just rear but seemed to spiral around while he was up on his hind legs; everything seemed to blur before my eyes, the light around us flickered like some joker was playing with the switches, and when Ex came down on all fours again my head was dancing.

'Sorry,' drawled Max, 'but that's the quickest way to take a small step forward.'

'What now Max?'

'We just went three weeks ahead; the quick way.'

There I am sitting at my desk again, and now the three J's are arriving. We all look pleased and I recognise that somehow Max has got us to the end of month sales meeting.

'Great result everyone.' That's me again. 'We did it, we hit that target and you guys have done a fantastic job.'

Everyone is glowing; you can see how pleased the three are.

'Thanks boss,' said Jeanne, 'it's nice to be appreciated.'

That's when the phone rang. Sitting behind Max I felt a cold tingle in my spine. I knew what was coming, but watched enthralled, as the scene that I had lived through all those years ago unfolded again in front of me.

'Hi Mr Boss,' I said to the telephone. The team sat forward expectantly.

'You've seen the figures, great. What do you think?' I wink at my team, smiling. But you could tell from the look that replaced the smile, and then by the tone in my voice, that the answer I got was not the one I was expecting.

'Oh … well thanks; yes I understand; thank you Sir, I will. Goodbye'.

The team looked incredulous. 'Wasn't he pleased?' asked Johnnie

'Yes, he said to congratulate you all on a good solid job.'

'Solid, is that the best he could say?'

'No he also said that the Southern team did their target plus 50% and that while he was pleased we had made the numbers, he was disappointed that we hadn't excelled like they had.'

It was like a cool breeze deflating a soufflé. The team's enthusiasm collapsed, and what had been a celebration became a dismal conclusion to our moment of glory.

'Don't seem like a happy ending there pardner.'

'No Max it wasn't, from hope to hell in 60 seconds

flat. I have never felt so disappointed and humiliated as I did at that moment.'

A short high pitched whine interrupted us, a bit like a quickly deflating balloon.

'Oh dear,' said Max.

'What's wrong?' I asked, then my senses began to reel.

'Sorry about that, I shouldn't let Ex eat cabbage.'

I put my hand over my face covering my nose and mouth; as I did Johnny stood up coughing.

'For goodness sake, Jimmy!'

'It wasn't me,' said Jimmy pulling a handkerchief from his pocket and cramming it over his nose as they both stared accusingly at Jenny, who blushed and stood protesting 'Not me either,' and left the room followed by the other two.

I looked quizzically at Max.

'Yes, I'm afraid that seems to be the one thing that can cross the space/time continuum thing.'

I remembered the incident, and watched as the young me opened a window fanning the air with my hand. At the time I thought it was nervous tension getting to one of the team, I never considered that it could have been an invisible flatulent horse from 14 years in the future.

'C'mon old bud,' said Max as he pulled on the reigns and turned us away from the scene. 'We may have unravelled one of the more odorous mysteries of mankind, but we also need to help you learn how you missed a trick with your management of the team. Let's go learn some lessons. Let's find out how you could have done better. Move 'em on.'

Part 2

Grunt and slash. A glistening blade gouges air and plunges into sweet soft flesh. A vein rips and spits its scarlet response into the face of the aggressor. That face, twisted with anguish and fury, shines a beacon of hatred at the prone and thrashing figure of the girl who is crying out and soon to die. Again: up, driving the blade, down and deep, down and deep, over and frenzied over again. At last the thrashing response of the victim quiets; life ebbs away leaving the murderer gasping from exertion and shaking with the adrenalin that is slowing in his veins. Blackness; surrounding, smothering blackness slips over the scene and steels all hope of light; silence wed to that blackness seals the moment as if filing it carefully out of sight.

Light and sound explodes. The stabbed girl is on her feet, hand in hand with her murderer. All around the silence is thrust violently aside as the exuberant applause of 500 people greets the actors who now come to the front of the stage and smiling, take their bows, visibly moved by the energetic response from their audience who are on their feet and chorusing approval.

'I'm in here somewhere!' I shout at Max over the noise as I point at the audience. 'We were all here, all the flatmates, this was a triumph for Janice. It was her first sell out. She turned this place from a sad disaster into a roaring success.'

'Exactly,' said Max, 'ever wonder how?'

'Not really, she's got that magic something.'

'Magic something?' snorted Max. Ex seemed to be looking over his shoulder at me with whatever the equine equivalent of disdain is, and as Max repeated my words they seemed suddenly inadequate.

'Well Max,' I tried to explain, 'you know some people just seem to be able to do it. I don't know how she did it, it was her personality or something, she is gifted; she always seems to be able to weave her magic, and has proved that over and again. That's why she runs her own successful business now.'

'Ok buddy, well let's see if we can work out just how she manages to "weave her magic" '. These last words were dealt slowly like cards in a poker hand, each laden with meaning; I could see from the wry smile on Max's face that he had a quite different interpretation of the reasons for Janice's success.

We were at the back of the auditorium and applause was still resounding around the place, the actors taking more bows. In front of us a young girl caught the eye of a young man, they were both standing and clapping wildly. 'Outrageously good,' he shouted and she laughed in agreement. 'Outrageously,' she said holding eye contact. Ex reared up on his hind legs and the lights flickered. This time I knew what was happening although I had to hold on to Max just as hard as before. I closed my eyes until we came down again with a bump and opened them to an empty theatre, dingy, dusty, littered and sad.

Part 3

'Back six months,' said Max.

'Yes this was how it began.' I climbed down from Ex and looked around the empty auditorium. 'I remember when Janice got the job. She came back to the flat one night so excited because she had the offer: General Manager for the Rodeo Theatre. We all came down here the next evening because none of us had ever been before and when we got here we found why – it was a dump. We came to see a comedy; I can't remember its title, it was terrible and the place was almost empty. It was just as it is now,' I pointed around me, 'scruffy, old battered seats, dirty – you didn't want to come a second time. I remember thinking you could see why they gave her the job; keeping it ticking over until it closed. I thought they were going to pull it down and sell the land to a supermarket or something. I didn't tell Janice that, she was so enthusiastic; despite the state of the place! It was as if she saw something different to the rest of us. But then who wouldn't be excited? She had just gone from junior manager to the boss in one quick move, she must have talked a great story at her interview.'

'Perhaps she did,' said Max, 'why don't we take a look?'

'What?'

'Janice's interview, it's just about to happen; get back up here pardner and we'll go take a look.'

'Hold on Max.' I stayed on my feet. 'Isn't it about time you gave me some explanation. You appear from nowhere when I haven't seen you for years,' I hold up a thumb, ' then you turn out to be invisible to everyone but me.' I'm counting the points on my fingers; 'You get me up on Ex and we seem to go time travelling to my past, and now it seems we can ride through walls and turn the clock backwards or forwards at the spin of a horse!'

'Why do you need an explanation, buddy? You seem to have it all figured out.'

'FIGURED OUT!'

'Don't shout buddy, no need to get excited.'

'But I am excited Max', I was gabbling. I could feel my face reddening. 'I'm talking to someone that doesn't exist and I'm seeing things that are impossible. Oh …' An idea awoke in my head. 'Hold on I get it, the bungee chord snapped didn't it? I didn't make it; I'm in a coma; that's it, this is all a dream. Where's the white light? Don't I get to walk towards a white light?'

'Head 'em up, just calm down. You're being ridiculous.'

'Ha, me ridiculous!' Ex was eyeing me.

'The bungee chord was just fine,' said Max 'everything has happened exactly as you remember. You've just found another slice to life.'

I paused, now what was this? 'Another slice to life.' I tasted these words and savoured my own sanity. I looked from Max to Ex and back to Max again. 'Another slice to life, Max?' I repeated the words slowly and deliberately, watching them carefully as they left my lips; nope, they still tasted the same, but perhaps I was insane.

'You need to accept that the world is not always the way you have assumed. We don't all see through the same eyes do we? **Our vision of the future defines what we believe is possible and so it may restrict or make possible what we actually achieve**. If you could only see this place as a dump destined for closure then you could never have done what Janice did; she let her imagination get to work and saw how it could be. In the same way, if you could only see that if your team worked hard it would be a good achievement to hit target, you excluded yourself from exceeding that target. Your vision was to hit target, not exceed it. Here at The Rodeo, Janice saw the possibility of success; she did see something different to the rest of you. That's what I mean by another slice to life. I'm going to show you what happened to Janice, and perhaps you will see another way in which the world has not always been what you assumed. Come on, let's keep movin'.'

I climbed back onto Ex feeling like a naughty schoolchild. 'Thanks Max,' I mumbled, deciding simply to give in to whatever this experience was. He flicked on the reigns and Ex cantered off through the back wall and up a flight of stairs. I yawned, oh yeah, seen it all before. On through a closed office door and there was Janice sitting opposite three rather dismal looking characters. They turned out to be a bank manager, a representative from a pension fund who owned a large share in the theatre and someone from the council. They were the interviewing panel and they weren't exactly humming with enthusiasm … but Janice was.

Part 4

'Yes Miss Sheriff,' drawled the dull manager from the council, shuffling in his seat and creasing even further the neglected brown corduroy jacket he was wearing, 'Please tell us how you feel you could improve things here at The Rodeo Theatre.'

Janice was shining, or so it seemed. She was smiling, leaning forward and looking each of them in the eye, one by one. She seemed to emit confidence as she explained exactly how she planned to reinvigorate the theatre and its employees.

'The change begins with Goals,' she began.

'Yes we have goals already,' interrupted the bank manager, her tight bun threatening to slice her scalp from her forehead if she moved too quickly. 'Our goal here is to bring this place back into profit.'

'I understand,' replied Janice positioning herself to face the bank manager, opening her hands and giving this person her full attention. The bank manager looked back unwavering, but to the invisible observer sitting on a horse next to a cowboy (unlikely but possible I suppose) there was a chink in the bank manager's demeanour that had not been there before.

'But the kind of goals I have in mind,' continued Janice, 'will, I believe, form a major part in the transformation that I am confident is possible.'

The immaculately suited pension fund manager lifted an eyebrow at the word transformation and in a soft Scottish lilt said, 'We are not looking for transformations, Miss Sheriff, just a profit.'

Janice's slight movement may not have been noticeable to the interviewing panel but, to me watching this, I saw her once again subtly reposition herself so that she now gave the new speaker her full attention. Looking directly into his eyes, with an open and friendly demeanour she replied, 'Profitability is at the centre of my plans. The goals that I recommend will, I believe, lead directly to strong profitability for the theatre. We must set goals that lead to profitability and alongside those goals we must have action plans. A goal will tell us where we want to be, but will be pointless without a plan of action to make the goal happen. That is why I have constructed a series of **SMART Goals and Action Plans** as part of my strategy for the regeneration of this theatre.'

The pension fund manager settled back in his chair, the look on his face was not unfriendly, it simply said, 'Tell me more'.

Janice proceeded to make a presentation that I guessed she had carefully prepared and rehearsed. 'I believe that we must create a series of goals that everyone in the team, and by that I mean all employees of the theatre and all stakeholders like yourselves, can clearly understand.'

'Those Goals must be **S specific**; by that I mean not open to interpretation; what is required is quite clear to anyone who hears that goal. Along with specific it must also be **M measurable**; this goes hand-in-hand with specific in that we make it clear how we will know when this goal has been achieved. When a goal is measurable anyone can tell whether we have achieved the goal or how far we have got towards it. I want to introduce specific and measurable goals because it would be easy for us to amble along with goals that are non-specific and, as a result, ineffective – they won't get achieved. Examples of non-specific goals would be: improve profits, increase tickets sales, provide better service or keep the theatre cleaner.'

'But our goals need more, to make them as powerful as possible. They must be **A achievable and agreed**; it must be possible to reach this goal since if we set crazy goals that we will never achieve then no one will take notice of them, the goal will be ignored or worse, become a de motivator because we are setting our team up to fail. This, however, is not such an easy thing to achieve because we must also make sure that our goals are stretching and not too easy, or else we under-perform. The team leader must make this difficult judgment, although I would suggest that it is done in consultation with the team so that the goal becomes agreed as well as achievable. If you give me this job that is exactly what I plan to do.'

'The goal must also be **R realistic and relevant**, that is it must be achievable with the available resources, knowledge and time, and further must clearly contribute to the overall aims of the organisation. Once it has passed these four tests then each Goal must be **T time bound,** meaning that there is a timescale for its completion, ideally a timeline with key points along the way and most definitely a finish time or date.

'This is what I mean by **SMART,** the process of making a vague goal focussed and effective.'

'Very interesting Miss Sheriff,' this was the bank manager now looking up from her notes and over the rim of her glasses. 'This sounds like a thorough process, but is it really necessary? Isn't this just fashionable theory that you read in a management book?'

'It is essential,' replied Janice her tone a little more direct. 'Without clear goals we have no direction and things will not be achieved.' Janice's eyes were bright as she made her point, her voice clear and steady. 'I did learn this originally as theory, but have put this concept into practice on a personal level and a business level. I set personal goals for my own development and achievement; I am sitting in front of you today because this job fits with one of my goals. **Without clear goals we lack the direction or insight to see how an opportunity fits the future we have planned; we don't see the relevance of things**. The goal provides focus, something to aim at, and with something to aim at you have a real chance of achieving what you seek.'

Janice's enthusiasm was infectious. I could see all three members of the interview panel gaining interest in what she was saying. The council representative was leaning forward, the bank manager was taking notes and the pension fund man was beginning to smile. Janice clearly believed every word she was saying, and that made those words even more persuasive.

'If you give me this job, I propose to involve the whole team in setting a series of SMART Goals that will lead us toward my vision of a successful future for The Rodeo Theatre. Then we will move toward action, goals are useless without action plans to make them happen. As well as SMART Goals we also need SMART Action Plans'.

'Aha SMART Action Plans, now we are getting to some nitty gritty,' said the pension fund man. 'I would very much like to hear about those.'

'Come on buddy,' it was Max talking to me now; we know what happens here, she gets the job, let's go find out what she did once she got started.'

'Yes good idea Max, I think I'm getting the idea of this hopping around in time now, where to next?'

'Two weeks ahead. Management meeting. Let's go'.

Part 5

I won't bore you with the detail of the spinning horse stuff that took place, but we were back in the auditorium of the theatre. On stage three chairs took centre position and in them sat Janice and two others, who turned out to be her Stage Manager and her Front of House Manager. The stage lights were on, bathing them in clean white light, while the auditorium was also partly lit so that it could be seen from the stage. I knew this was Janice's sense of theatre at work; she would get her management team together on the most emotive spot in the place, centre stage, in order to discuss how they would change the future of this theatre for the better.

In the dimmed light you didn't see the dirt and the shabby detail, instead the positive qualities of this proud old theatre came to life. The decoration appeared elegant and the atmosphere charming – it would be a tragedy to lose this to another glass and chrome shopping experience, but then if the customers don't want it, what point is there in simply hanging on to history? Luckily Janice didn't seem to share this view, she was talking to her team.

'So that's what I mean by SMART Goals, and I want us to set some.'

I guessed the other two had received the same presentation that the interview board got but they did not look enthused. Nigel, The Stage Manager, was a jeans, sweatshirt and trainer man, whilst Sheila, the Front of House Manager, elegant in an old-fashioned way, looked tired and cynical. It seemed that even Janice's enthusiasm had failed to win over this pair, who appeared to be assessing their new young boss with a fiercely critical eye.

'I don't wish to be rude,' said Nigel, 'but we have heard this kind of stuff before, it makes no difference. We talk about it and make plans, but this won't get over the fact that people just don't come to the provincial theatre these days, they sit at home and watch television.'

'We've tried everything,' added Sheila. 'Promotions, different types of show, changing the image, it has made no difference. The person you replaced was full of enthusiasm, just like you, but he only lasted six months before it got the better of him. And we, Nigel and I, have to carry on and keep this place afloat while another new person arrives, drags us through a whole bunch of new ideas until they give up and go. No offence intended Janice, but we've seen it all before.'

'I appreciate your honesty,' replied Janice, 'but something has to change here or this theatre will close. We can't continue to make losses for much longer before the Board has no choice but to close us down. Do you agree?'

'Yes,' admitted Sheila, 'but ...'

'Hold on Sheila' said Janice, 'I accept the points you have made and I ask you both just to co-operate with me in this planning exercise and if, at the end, you still think it's a waste of time then we can talk again. Do we have a deal?'

Nigel and Sheila looked at each other and shrugged. 'Ok,' they both said; it seemed clear that neither were difficult people, just deeply frustrated with their circumstances and lack of success.

'I would like us to create some SMART Goals together,' said Janice, but we must do this with care. We need first to understand exactly where we are now and in particular what are our strengths and weaknesses. So I would like us to carry out a **SWOT analysis**.' Sheila raised her eyebrows and Nigel crossed and uncrossed his legs, but both kept quiet.

'I want us to consider our **S strengths, W weaknesses, O opportunities and T threats.** That information will help us identify relevant Goals which we can then make SMART.'

Janice produced three notepads with pens, giving one each to Nigel and Sheila and keeping one for herself. 'Let's begin,' she said. 'I want us all to think about the theatre's Strengths. Try to write down five and then we can compare notes'.

Watching this was interesting; we saw their behaviour change. The three of them, on stage, became actors in their own production. Max and I called it 'Saving The Rodeo'. Janice got them involved in the SWOT analysis and their resistance diminished as they turned their attention to the task. Once they had shared their lists of strengths and removed the duplicates, they had a total of 10 between them. Then they worked their way through Weaknesses, Opportunities and Threats with similar results. They had good debate around what was or was not an item in each category, and we saw an engagement between them that had not been present during the awkward start to the meeting. At the end when Janice summarised their discussion and led them to the subject of Goals, the atmosphere was quite changed for the better. Where before they would have been casting around for ideas for Goals now these ideas were rising out of the SWOT analysis.

Here is an example of what they agreed and how they got there.

They began with a question, considered the relevant Strengths, Weaknesses, Opportunities and Threats; then constructed a Goal.

The question they chose was **how can we improve ticket sales?**

Strengths (What advantages do we have? What can we do better? What unique resources do we have? What do people see as our strength?)

Thousands of people know who and where we are.
Thousands of people have been through our doors over the years.
We have many names and addresses.
People recognise that there is no other auditorium like ours in town.

Weaknesses (What can we improve? What should we avoid? What do people see as our weaknesses?)

We don't have much dialogue with our customers past or present.
We don't attract enough younger people.
People think we are expensive (but we are not compared to many other entertainments).

Opportunities (Where are they? What changes in technology, society, local events, etc. could bring opportunity? Can eliminating weaknesses bring opportunities?)

We share customers with other non-competitive businesses.
We are not expensive compared to many other entertainments (but people think we are).
There is a local arts festival that brings many people into the area but we don't have any links with it.

Threats (What obstacles do we face? What are the competition doing that is better than us? Have our customers' requirements for service changed?)

Our reputation has gone down because not all shows have been good.
The cinemas are better at marketing than we are.
Other forms of entertainment are increasingly competing with us.

In discussing these they agreed that they could improve ticket sales by finding new ways to talk with prospective customers. The **SMART Goal** that came from this was:

Find three new ways of talking to customers within the next two weeks and create 200 extra ticket sales per week from these three new methods, within three months.

The SWOT analysis helped them find three SMART Goals in total, the other two being about improving the customer experience on show nights and improving the cleanliness and repair of the auditorium.

We had been watching for an hour when the meeting came to a close. Sheila and Nigel had gone from outright scepticism to guarded interest and this seemed to have been achieved through their involvement in the SWOT analysis and Goal setting exercise. At the end of the meeting Janice pressed on the opportunity she had created.

'I am pleased with the three SMART Goals that we have created,' she said ' we are now half way toward completing our plan. **Our Goals are useless without activity to make them happen. Alongside each SMART**

Goals we need a SMART Action Plan, and to achieve this I want us to involve the entire team.'

'Who do you mean?' asked Sheila.

'I mean everyone that works for us,' replied Janice.

'Surely you don't mean *everyone!*' Nigel looked dismayed.

'I do,' said Janice,' They are our Hidden Treasure. I mean everyone.'

'Bar staff, cleaners, stage hands?' questioned Nigel.

'Yes Nigel, every one of those employees is a resource with potential to offer. I want us to hold a meeting with everyone and I want them involved in thinking about our new Goals and creating our Smart Action Plans.'

'Not possible,' said Sheila, 'many of them are part time, and we just can't get them all here together.'

'Can't?' asked Janice.

It's interesting how often I have given into that argument, I thought, as Janice dealt with the 'can't'. She certainly saw possibilities where I knew I would have been guilty of accepting other people's barriers. And it was just five days later that she held her meeting; although to Max and me it seemed only minutes away!

Part 6

Before we got to that gathering of the theatre staff, Max stopped our travels to ask me what I was learning.

'Good question, Max. So much has been happening that I haven't thought about that. Since you ask, I think I am learning that Janice was **creating a sense of direction and purpose** better than anything I ever did.

I had goals but never as defined as Janice's, and they were never constructed with such clear focus. If you remember what was happening with my sales team, we had a goal which was 'to hit target', and I accepted that goal from my boss. I never questioned whether it was the right goal and we certainly didn't create SMART Action Plans. Everyone just went away to do their own job, I suppose our plan was to try harder than they had done before. I can see now how much more effective we could have been by challenging my boss's goal and making our own SMART Goal. I suspect that what a SWOT analysis would have done would be to give us more options. If we had constructed a SMART Action Plan for each of us I bet that we too would have been exceeding the boss's goal, like they did in the Southern region. They had seen possibilities where I had not.'

'I think so too,' agreed Max, 'so why don't we go and look at what Janice did next?'

And so it was that we found ourselves for a final time in the theatre's auditorium, but this time we were not alone; instead we were accompanied by the staff for whom this was clearly a novelty. There was some giggling amongst a few who looked as if they had never sat in the theatre before, whilst others were looking around with a condescending expression on their faces. I guessed that some were not happy to be mixing like this with those they felt to be below them, while others were enjoying this elevation to significance.

Janice was alone on stage, her two senior managers seated amongst their people. 'Good evening everyone. I appreciate the particular effort that some of you have made to be here,' started Janice. 'I want to ask for your help. I'm sure you are all aware that The Rodeo

Theatre is not doing well. Those of you who have worked here for a long time will see that we are not as busy as we used to be; that is something we must change if we are to survive. I ask you to look around you at this proud old place.' Janice raised a hand and directed everyone's eyes around the theatre. 'Take a look at it.' Her audience did just that, running their eyes over the Edwardian interior, the balconies, the curtains, the highly decorated ceiling. 'What you see is a tired old friend who needs our help, and indeed we need the theatre's help because our jobs depend on it. Times have changed and we haven't kept up, now we are paying the price. My management team and I are determined to put new plans together that will make a difference. And that's where we need you!' Her two hands were now outstretched toward her audience.

Each of the three SMART Goals agreed by the management team were projected onto a screen set in the middle of the stage. Janice explained the meaning and importance of **SMART Action Plans** like this:

'Imagine making a New Year's Resolution (Goal) like 'I am going to lose weight this year'. It's not SMART and unlikely to be effective.

Try 'I'm going to lose 6kgs in the next 8 weeks.' This is SMART but with no plan on how you're going to achieve it, it's not going to happen.

Perhaps you try a bit harder with a plan but your plan is poorly formed, 'I will do more exercise and improve my diet'. Destined for failure isn't it? It's too vague, not SMART.

SMART Action Plans create the best chance of activity happening that will make a difference. **S specific**: Who and what; **M measurable:** How to measure progress and success; **A achievable:** Can I do it? **R realistic**: Will I do it? **T time bound:** When will I do it?

And this is where it gets personal. **To make action plans SMART they must be allocated to those who will carry out the actions**. In fact a SMART Action Plan is most powerful when it is shared with someone else who undertakes to hold you to it. Now we could form a much more effective Goal and Action Plan.

Goal: 'I'm going to lose 6kgs in the next 8 weeks.'

Action Plan: 'I will exercise at the gym for 30 minutes three times a week and restrict my calorie intake to 1500 per day.'

Then Janice showed the four lists that the management team had created under the headings Strengths, Weaknesses, Opportunities and Threats and explained that they may find this a useful starting point for creating Action Plans for saving The Rodeo. Janice asked everyone to divide into small groups to consider the outcome of the SWOT analysis and come up with ideas for Action Plans that would help achieve the three SMART goals. Nigel and Sheila were tasked with moving from group to group, helping and encouraging.

Much to Sheila and Nigel's surprise everyone did get involved. Little groups set themselves up around the auditorium and became busy talking. As Max and I watched this we saw people at first looking a little awkward and then as group after group formed and began the job in hand, everyone became involved.

'Ok pardner, just one more little trip before we go.'

'Aren't we going to stay and see how they get on?' I asked.

'They get on just fine, but I want to show you how

this gathers pace, how it keeps going beyond this meeting and draws other people in. Come on, ride 'em in.' Max grazed his spurs over Ex's flank and in seconds we were gone.

Part 7

Our final destination turned out to be to a smart wine bar in town. A group of four were sitting together. Max left Ex at the door and we sat by them to hear their conversation. They were the lighting technician from The Rodeo, one of the stage hands and his girlfriend and a lady who was in charge of make up. They were talking about the meeting at the theatre, the same one we had just left. This must have been an hour or so later, which Max confirmed.

'You are so lucky,' said the stage hand's girlfriend. At my work they never ask us anything, just tell us what to do.'

'Yes, it's certainly a change for us,' said the make up lady 'but finding the ideas is something else.'

The lighting manager took a piece of paper from his pocket and read, 'Here is the Goal again, 'To find three new ways of talking to customers within two weeks.' What about us all walking up and down the high street carrying sandwich boards and talking to people?'

'I hope you are joking,' replied the make up lady, 'that's definitely not my job. We need something better than that.'

Just then their drinks arrived, 'One bottle of Rioja and three glasses,' said the bar manager who was waiting on the group, 'and one Cappuccino.' With the drinks he gave them a receipt along with a glossy leaflet offering a midweek ticket discount at the local multiscreen cinema.

'Why have you given us that?' asked the lighting tech.

'We're running a promotion with the cinema,' replied the bar manager.

'Is it successful?' said the stage hand's girlfriend.

'Too early to tell. We're meant to get free tickets for the staff depending on how many people use these vouchers when they book their tickets. We're hoping they might run some promotions here and forge a real link so that we would get more customers from it.'

The group were looking at each other and experiencing an 'aha' moment,

'How would you feel about making that kind of link with The Rodeo Theatre?' asked the lighting tech.

'I don't think they'd be interested,' replied the bar manager, 'they're far too snooty for us.'

'Ever been there?'

'Yes, when I was a kid. My gran took me to the pantomime, but I haven't been since.'

The conversation continued with the group from the theatre introducing themselves to the bar manager who rapidly began to change his view about the theatre. By the end of the conversation they had agreed on just how a promotion could work between a wine bar (or a restaurant) and the theatre to the benefit of all concerned. By the time a second bottle of wine was finished the group had their proposal for a **SMART Action Plan**. It read:

To make a link with 10 bars or restaurants, within two weeks, to be called Rodeo Friends. To offer benefits to customers of the Rodeo Friends who book theatre tickets, promote theatre events through Rodeo Friends and promote the Friends through the theatre.

They agreed that this action would help bring about the SMART Goal to

'Find three new ways of talking to customers within two weeks and then to create 200 extra ticket sales per week from these three new methods within three months'.

'And that,' said Max, 'is an insight into how Janice led the transformation of The Rodeo. She got her management team involved with SMART Goals which led them to share a vision and direction. Even though at first they were disapprovin' she got the whole team of employees to engage in creating SMART Action Plans to make the SMART Goals happen. She got 'em movin'. What came back from the employees was a wide mix of ideas, like the one we just saw created, and from those they were able to allocate a series of SMART Action Plans that everyone understood and felt a part of. Janice had got the employee team involved so that when it came to putting those plans into action everyone was thinking about it and being supportive. With this came new ideas and new thinking that injected a fresh energy and approach that saved The Rodeo.'

'Incredible Max. I knew Janice when all this was happening to her, but we didn't see much of her at the flat. She was always at work and when she wasn't she seemed to be in her room sleeping. Now I see what she was doing, I have a better understanding of how she created her success. There is nothing here that I could not have done with my work challenges, I just didn't know how.'

'What do you think about Janice's "magic something" now?'

'What?'

'When I asked you earlier, you put her success down to having that "magic something". Is that still what you think?'

'I see your point, thank you Max. There is no magic, is there? She knew better than I did how to make things happen, she was using knowledge and techniques that I could have used.'

'She sure was buddy. I guess our work here is complete. Time to move on.'

'Are you taking me home now Max?'

'Not if you want to learn more, buddy.'

'More?'

'Well you sounded pretty desperate when you called me back, and I can show you all you need to know to git you out of that hole you're in.'

'You can Max?'

'Summarise your problem for me.'

'My problem is that I just don't seem able to be anything better than average. I do ok, but never great. I need to know the things I'm missing.'

'I know bud, I know. Do you think what you have learned from Janice will help?'

'No doubt it will Max.'

'Then let me show you more. Success is waitin' at the end of our ride. By the time we've finished you will know just how to get people to perform to their very best and as a manager, that's how you achieve outstanding success. This journey is not about how you get people to work together, that's team working, and I see you already know how to make that happen. This journey is about how to get your people to perform to the Max. Ready to go?'

'Yes.' I laughed. I had stopped trying to work all this out; I was ready to go. Allowing myself to dive into this adventure with Max was a liberating feeling. 'Head 'em out Max,' and as my inhibitions slipped away I found myself dressed like Max: a Stetson on my head, six shooters at my hips, cowhide jacket, leather chaps, jingling spurs.

'Hey,' shouted Max with a smiling shout, 'just like old times now, buddy; soon we'll be livin' high and wide.'

'Yee Ha,' we whooped in unison, 'count 'em out, ride 'em in,' and we waved our Stetsons in the air. Ex threw back his handsome mane, gave a deep snort and strode forward into a velvety black space that opened up in front of us.

'Where to now Max?' I yelled, as I held on tight.

Learning Questions

1. Why did my team fail to excel?
2. What was the first step that Janice took toward her success at The Rodeo (before setting Goals)?
3. How did Janice deal with those who implied that it couldn't be done by saying 'we've seen it all before'?
4. What activity did Janice get her management team to undertake to help with creating meaningful goals?
5. How did Janice begin to satisfy the Group Needs described by Helen in HIDDEN TREASURE?
6. What do you think Janice hoped to achieve by involving all staff members in creating action plans?

Learning Summary – Goal Setting and Action Planning

Setting Goals is about clearly envisioning an outcome and making sound plans to achieve it.

Without goals we lack direction; without plans we lack impetus.

To be effective both Goals and Action Plans should be S (specific), M (measurable), A (achievable), R (realistic) and T (time bound).

Analysing your S(strengths), W(weaknesses),

O(opportunities) and T (threats) helps understand a current situation and develop ideas for goals and action plans.

Actions must be allocated to, and accepted by, individuals.

FORWARD MOTION (MANAGING PERFORMANCE)

Part 1

The roar was unexpected, but not as unexpected as the vibration between my legs. We were moving fast, faster than a horse could run. My eyes focused, I was looking through something; something that was sitting on my head! A slow panic was blooming within me and then I heard Max talking in my ear – his deep voice was distorted as if heard through a telephone line.

'Sorry about the bumpy landing,' he crackled. 'Ex missed his footing just before we left and it brought us in at a funny angle.'

Yet again I had nothing to say. This day had already bombarded me with so much and now there was more. In my head for the umpteenth time today a voice was asking, 'What's happening now?'

'You ok?' asked Max's disembodied voice, by which time my senses had achieved enough of a balance to realise that he and I were on a motorbike and I was hearing his crackly voice through the intercom inside a helmet.

'You might have warned me, Max,' I shouted, as countryside flew past us and I clung on hard. 'Sorry bud,' he drawled, 'I forgot how slow your imagination has become since the old days.'

'Bog off Max.'

'No problem.'

We roared around a bend the bike dipping, Max whooping and me about to be sick. To my relief we slowed and turned between a pair of large ornate gates, passing a sign I did not have time to read, and cruising slowly along a lengthy drive, through woodland and then open country, toward a large sprawling building. My relief was complete when Max brought the bike to a halt on a gravel parking area and turned off the engine.

'Max explain please.'

'The next stage in our journey; we've gone forward.'

'Forward?'

'In time.'

'In time?'

'Doesn't usually have this effect.'

'Effect?'

'The journey seems to have stolen your words and just left you with mine'.

He was a smug cowboy sometimes, that was annoying, but now I noticed that he was no longer a cowboy and, for that matter, neither was I.

'Max you were always a cowboy now you're a …' I stepped off the bike and looked at Max: black leathers, big black shiny bike, black helmet 'you're a … biker.'

'You too, old friend.'

I looked down at myself to recognise that Max and I were dressed identically.

'How come, Max?'

'We went forward Bud. Ex only comes along when we go backwards from your start point, when we come forwards he changes into this; Max opened his palms in front of him to indicate the bike. It was certainly a handsome machine, a worthy mechanical equivalent to the handsome horse.

'Ok Max, it's not helping me to question too much, I'll just go with it.'

Max nodded

'So where are we?' I asked.

Max pointed behind me and I turned to take in the surroundings for the first time. A delightful old building, three stories in height, ivy growing across its face, colourful flowers in beds to the front, and modern extensions tastefully extending at either side. Above the door an elegant sign read 'Excelsior Hotel'. It looked expensive.

'Let's go' said Max as he removed his helmet and climbed off the bike.

'Can we be seen when we're off the bike Max?'

'No, as long as we wear our leathers we remain invisible. We can have no impact on what happens here, we can only watch and listen.'

'And this is my future, Max?'

'It could be. But right now we aren't going to see you, we are going to see one of your friends.'

Max led the way toward the main door and I followed.

'When is this Max?'

'14 years ahead of your start time, you will be 51 when we see you here.'

Part 2

'I am outraged. Outraged!'

Through the large double doors swept a flurry of hair, fur and expensive perfume, all balanced on heels probably a little too high for a lady of this age. Arms and hips were swinging as she flounced over the hotel threshold and pointed at a large black vehicle, which immediately began to glide gracefully toward her. In her wake appeared a short man (stooped shoulders, thin moustache, trilby hat) being led by the most miniature of poodles on a slender lead as it trotted after its Mistress.

'Hold on Leo,' he grumbled as it strained its slender neck against a jewelled collar.

Max and I both stared at the poodle that had been clipped into the shape of a coffee table, except that its little thin tail was almost bald apart from the hair at the end, which was shaped into a pompom and dyed pink.

Behind all three appeared a tall gangly man in black lounge suit.

'Madame, Madame, if you pliz,' there was an edge of desperation in his strong French accent.

'Permettez moi to correct the matter, eet was not meant as an insult.'

The perfumed dervish spoke no further words, but instead communicated with her handbag, a stout and large designer accessory, which now appeared at head height swinging in a circular motion, like an athlete's hammer, toward the tall man's head. Fortunately for him he ducked in time and, fortunately for the lady's companion, who was now left in the line of fire, he was just too short for the bag to make contact with his head, although sufficiently tall for it to sweep off his hat. It span through the air like a graceful but unambitious frisbee, as it journeyed only a few feet. The fear of impending concussion had been sufficient to cause the shorter man to let go of the dog lead and the most miniature of poodles had begun to trot freely when the spinning trilby landed squarely on top of it, leaving only four tiny feet and the pink pompom on display. The frightened animal then scampered blindly down the driveway with the short man in pursuit. A uniformed hotel doorman rushed to assist the outraged lady into her conveyance which set off following the short man, following the animated trilby.

Meanwhile the tall man held his head in his hands and groaned; then turning on his heels he roared 'Melvin' and headed back into the hotel.

'Come on' said Max, 'time for us to follow.'

Part 3

The tall man was the General Manager of the hotel who cursed loudly in French as he strode along a service corridor and threw open an office door. Inside another man sat behind a desk staring at a computer screen. The General Manager's arms exploded in a blur of gesticulation and he began to shout, the man behind the desk starting in surprise. As the General Manager heaped abuse upon abuse, the other man's face reddened and he stood and began shouting back.

'Monsieur Gibbon you are an imbecile,' screamed the General Manager.

'Don't shout at me you false frenchie.'

'Oy mate, 'oo you calling false?' (General Manager now turned cockney.)

'You're from blinking Barking you git.'

'You just lost us one of our best customers you idiot.'

'I've been in here all morning, I haven't done anything'

'Your staff, idiot – you are Food and Beverage Manager remember?'

'Half my staff ARE idiots, you can't get good staff in this god forsaken area.'

The shouting matched continued with intensity, volume rising. During all this I realised with some shock that I was looking at my old friend Mel, as in Mel who looked like a bronzed god and never ceased to attract the ladies, except this Mel was bald, lined, bowed … old! And I mean old beyond his years. Max had warned me that we were 14 years ahead and that meant Mel would be about 50, but he looked 60. His skin was blotchy, there were dark drooping rings under his once handsome eyes and his clothes looked shabby, certainly not the same Mel who was once so particular about his appearance.

I looked around his office surprised that Mel was not the General Manager. I always saw Mel as a man who would lead the way in whatever he did. Mel was a winner. The walls displayed charts, targets and procedures, this looked like the office of a man who was focussed on where he was going; so how come he didn't appear to be getting anywhere?

'What do you expect me to do?' shouted Mel with eyes bulging, face a bilious purple, spittle at the corner of his mouth, 'Look around you: we have targets, procedures, visions statements coming out of our damned ears – it's the staff. They're useless.'

The General Manager had at least gained control of himself and responded in a cold and controlled voice (that clearly came from nearer Barking than Boulogne) 'You're fired'. Mel, stopped his ranting and stared. 'Fired, mon ami,' repeated the General Manager as if re-establishing his French credentials. 'Collect your belongings monsieur and go. Maintenant!' He briskly turned on his heel, as if dismissing Mel from his thoughts, and left. Mel picked up the nearest thing to hand which happened to be a calculator and hurled it at the door that had closed behind the General Manager. 'Sometimes you just can't win,' he shouted as it slammed into the wooden door frame and shattered. As this happened Mel staggered and clutched his chest, his breathing becoming shallow. He put one hand on the desk to steady himself and appeared to be sitting down, but instead slid to the floor beside the chair ending with his head wedged awkwardly against a filing cabinet and his feet twitching.

'Max he's having some kind of fit. Do something.'

'We can't old bud, we can't be heard or seen.'

I knelt down by Mel; his breathing was shallow. My hands went through him when I tried to touch him. I looked at Max in desperation.

'Time to go Bud, we've seen enough.'

'No Max, I can't leave Mel like this.'

'You can't help him either.'

'I can Max, you said I'm invisible only when I wear these leathers, I can take them off and go for help.'

'That's a bad idea old friend.'

I wasn't listening, I was determined to remove the

leathers and save Mel. The problem was that as I had not put them on, I had to work out how to get them off and that wasn't easy. I managed to get half way through the job, hopping about on one leg with the damn things half on and half off before I tipped over and crashed into a cupboard. A calm voice that was not Max said 'What, my friend, are you doing here?'

I looked up from the floor to see Mel standing over me.

'Mel, you're ok!'

Then I saw his body lying still behind the desk.

'Seems like I'm moving on,' he replied 'who's your friend?'

'Oh this is Max. But what's happening to you?'

Mel, or the Mel who was standing over me, was beginning to fade.

'No idea. You know how much I hated arguments or any kind of unpleasantness, now it feels like I have somewhere good to go,' he smiled, his voice getting fainter. And then he faded completely; he vanished. Except his body was still lying on the floor.

I looked at Max. 'He's dead, old bud. Reckon he had a heart attack. He just passed this way on his journey. There's nothing left in there now,' he pointed at Mel's body, 'and it really is time for us to go. There is no more for us to learn here.'

I clambered to my feet shaken and curious to understand what had happened to Mel. We made our way back to the bike and Max explained, 'Mel was a victim of stress, that's why he aged so much. Managing people can be tough when you don't know how, and persistent high-level stress attacks your health. Poor Mel never learned how to Manage Performance, and so he faced persistent frustration. He would set objectives and make plans thinking that would fix it, but he was wrong. Too often the people he managed didn't achieve those targets or stick to the plans; try as he might, real success would allude him and failure would haunt him. He was good at planning but never mastered how to focus the performance of his team members so that they successfully put the plans into action. He was a nice guy but he soaked frustration up inside and it took its toll'.

Poor Mel. What a turn up for the books, I thought.

'Come on,' Max was sitting on the bike and inviting me to get on. 'Let's cheer ourselves up. Let's take a look at you'.

Part 4

Red laser beams criss-crossed ahead of us, Mel brought the bike to a halt in front of them. He must have sensed my question before I asked it, 'We have to wait until they turn green; if you try to drive through the engine cuts'.

Beyond the lasers the road that crossed in front of us was busy, but the cars weren't cars. They at first looked like cars but the shape was different, rounded with no obvious front and, more importantly, not touching the ground but gliding over the surface. I realised that the outraged lady had climbed into one of these outside the hotel.

'It's Newtech,' said Mel, 'Newtech formally replaced oldtech two years ago now. If you've got wheels you take second place, can only travel on certain roads and when you do they're hell because they don't maintain those roads anymore.'

'What are they, Mel?'

'They're what replaced cars. They run on refracted light, travel on designated pathways and are guided by the Road System.'

'Refracted light?'

'Light travels at about 186,000 miles per second. Someone worked out that if you stop it with a certain type of filter it creates massive amounts of energy. It's called refracted fission. It caused a real fuss. All the oil rich countries found that oil no longer had any value and the world got endless free energy and loads of Newtech stuff. Cars were one of the first things to change and almost unlimited energy allowed the hover principle to be developed and replace wheels.'

'And what's the Road System?'

'It's a satellite controlled positioning technology all managed through a central point. You log your Newtech into the system, tap in your desired destination and sit back.'

'Nothing else?'

'Nothing. No driver, no controls, simplified engine taking less space, it changed the whole design of cars to focus away from the driver and onto what passengers do while they travel.'

The lasers turned green and Mel eased the bike onto the main road.

'But you're going to see soon enough,' crackled Mel through the helmet intercom, 'it's what you do in this place in time. You run a Newtech centre.'

'Run it?'

'Yes, you're the boss'.

I would have punched the air had I not been on the back of the bike. Me the boss, yes!

On our wheels we travelled along the road keeping to a clearly marked lane in which there were no other vehicles. Bumping over potholes, we were gawped at by passengers in the Newtechs. We were a curiosity and we were headed to see me 15 years ahead. This time I was prepared, I knew what was happening and was looking forward to the experience, although with some trepidation. Would I look as rough as Mel? Would I be keeling over and breathing my last as I watched? These thoughts were forming themselves as we arrived. This time Mel did not observe any niceties driving the bike straight at a fancy glass wall, which we passed through without impact and into a brightly lit display area.

Part 5

This place was warm and friendly. The people around couldn't see us but we could see smiling faces of both customers and staff. We were clearly in some kind of sales area. I was expecting to see the Newtech pods on display but instead the space was dominated by what looked like fittings and fixtures; my first impression was more of a high tech furniture showroom crossed with a computer store.

On one side, almost as an afterthought were three Newtech pods, each of a different size. 'It's not about the pods anymore, it's about what goes inside 'em,' explained Mel.

'Come on. We've arrived just in time,' and leaving the bike, visible only to us, we walked into a side room where I was greatly relieved to see a reasonably fit looking me leading a meeting.

'Welcome to this quarterly review meeting.' the other me said. 'Same format as usual, I will ask each of you to report on your department's performance and what you have done to improve it. I remind you that **Managing Performance is essentially about managing people. In other words, leadership;** we must work on the basis that our people have high capability and it is our role as managers to help them perform to their best. Where they do not achieve, we must look for the reasons within ourselves. Marion, tell us about the New Ownership department.'

Marion was a short efficient lady. She stepped neatly to a display board and produced a simple bar chart showing an upward trend. 'I am delighted to tell you that we are succeeding in our objective to attract more pod sales and registrations. The changes that I have made in the last three months are about **communication of expectations**. I realised that my team did not fully understand the standards that were required around all of their work and I resolved this with a team exercise. I got them to make a **list of the tasks that they feel are the most important part of our work;** we had a meeting where I explained what I wanted and a second meeting three days later when they came with their lists of tasks. Those lists covered everything that was important, I didn't have to add a thing and we were all surprised at how long the final list was. Next I asked the team to help me **set acceptable standards around those tasks,** to **set two types of standard for each task** on the list. The first standard was **Quantity** and we agreed that this meant how much, how many or at what speed in relation to the task; so when we considered the task of recording customers details on a datasheet, we asked how many datasheets should we expect in a week from each assistant and how long it should take to complete one with the customer. The second type of standard was **Quality**, and we agreed that this meant how we would decide if a task had been done well, so to continue with the example of the customer details we asked whether every piece of information required had been gained and added to the form, whether it had been completed legibly.

The interesting thing was that although I'm sure this all sounds dull to you, it wasn't to the team because this is their day to day work. It made me realise that **everyone wants to do a good job and when they know what good looks like they become more focussed on making it happen.** An unexpected outcome is that team members are having conversations amongst themselves about maintaining standards, whereas previously if something wasn't right I was the only person who would have said anything. I think that's because they played a part in creating those standards so they understand them and have taken ownership of them. As a result of this exercise standards have raised, the attitude amongst the team has improved, and guess what,' Marion turned and pointed at her chart, 'our figures are going up.'

'Thank you Marion,' this was me talking now. I noticed a little grey appearing in my hair, but I looked at ease and becoming rather distinguished, I thought. 'Your figures certainly have improved, there can be no doubt that you've led a change for the better and you have made these results happen. Congratulations, excellent work.'

Marion was not a demonstrative person, but you could see her glowing with pride as she returned to her seat.

'Martin, let's turn our attentions to the Design and Supply department.'

The second person to report was a bright eyed smartly dressed character, clearly full of energy. He smiled, looked everyone in the eye and said, 'Do you mind if I report from my seat, I have no chart to show you but instead I have some hand-outs that I will ask you to look at in a moment. It's been a busy few months for us. We have a whole new range of interiors using the latest NASA technology, so now pods can include a full bathroom or the model 3 boardroom or the series 2 pod cinema. Our focus has been helping the team to meet the standards – we already have a whole series of quantity and quality standards, but with each new product range and advance in technology we have to **focus on making sure that our team members are able to meet those standards**. We went back to thinking about team coaching and looked at every team member's strengths and weaknesses. We made a **skills matrix** with a full list of the most important tasks that the team undertakes down one side, the names of all team members along the top and then in the boxes this created we assessed each team member's strengths for each skill on a scale of 1 to 10. After that we could see the weak points and encouraged coaching between team members; where I had a team member with a strength I got that person to coach those with a weakness. We also used external coaching from specialists and suppliers to bring individual ability levels up to what was needed to do a great job. One effect has been to get team members looking forward to product changes rather than resisting, in fact getting excited about them and so doing a great job in presenting them to customers and giving advice.'

Martin handed round two sheets of paper clipped together, 'Here you can see a full schedule of product changes over the last three months, our figures for sales against each, and that's compared with our figures against comparable models for the previous three months. You will see that they're all up and I believe that's because I have a capable motivated team who enjoy getting their job done to a high standard. On the second page you will see the skills matrix that we created, tasks listed down the left hand side, team members across the top of the page, and beginning and end of quarter assessments of individual skill levels with each task – all showing an improvement. This quarter has had **people really thinking about their own development and working at i**t, they have enjoyed it and I'm sure that's why we're making progress.'

'I have no doubt Martin,' the fifty one year old me replied. 'Marion showed us just how she has **improved her team's understanding of what is expected** and you have showed us how you have **helped your team to meet expectations**; you've also done a fantastic job. Now I turned to the third member of the management team, 'Margaret how about the Performance Department?'

Margaret gave the impression that she would be more at home in a workshop, she looked a practical lady, simply sitting in her place to speak.

'As you know we have a continued challenge with the increasing efficiency of Pod manufacture. They go wrong less often so we come to rely more and more on refitting. Consequently it has become particularly important for us to work closely with Martin's department. My focus in the last quarter has been about **checking and monitoring**. We have been used to quantity and quality standards for a long time, my technicians are paid on the basis of hours taken for jobs and the quality of work achieved. But I have learned that **it is not enough to set good standards and to ensure the ability of team members to achieve those standards**. The manager cannot then afford to retire to her office and disappear behind a computer screen.

I think this is about the fallibility of human nature: **if left alone even the best team members will underperform and the weakest will most certainly run into trouble quickly**. I decided to speak with the team about this so we also held a meeting but ours was to discuss what level of monitoring would be most useful. I thought I would begin the meeting by telling the team how I benefited from being monitored – when I'm feeling tired and tempted to give in it is helpful to know that someone else will be checking what I'm doing both for quantity and quality. That knowledge doesn't allow me to succumb to the temptation to cut corners, I only have a problem with it if that monitoring is unreasonable or so time consuming that it gets in the way of achieving my work. You can imagine that this led to a thorough discussion at the end of which we all agreed that it was necessary to monitor all tasks and team members to some degree. We went on to look at a list of the key tasks that each of us must complete on a daily and weekly basis and decide how often and by whom the task should be monitored. For many we agreed on an occasional dip check, to see if all was ok, with others we agreed daily or weekly checking of output; with some tasks we agreed that it should be checked on every single occasion. By the end we had agreed how each task would be monitored. We have found two particular results from this: the first was that many more errors were picked up before they caused a problem and second that output has increased. When we discussed this second point we agreed that this was because we knew that someone would be monitoring our work so we became a little more focussed on getting it done within the quality standards. You will all be aware that our measured efficiencies and profitability have risen for the third quarter in a row.'

'Indeed they have Margaret,' the other me responded, 'your department's performance has been outstanding. Between the three of you we have achieved a first rate focus on managing performance and as a result we are doing more, more profitably. We must congratulate ourselves; recognise that we did this, this management team, we made this happen through our behaviour. If we were failing we would have to take it on the chin and accept our responsibility, equally as we are succeeding we must pat ourselves on the back and say 'Well done'. Marion you **set and communicated quantity and quality standards for all keys tasks in a way that all team members understood and accepted.** Martin you **made sure that your team members had the skills and knowledge to be able to meet those standards**, and Margaret you **made sure that all was kept on track through**

effective monitoring. The result of all this is that we are travelling towards our objectives, our plans are working, we are achieving a **mix of Goal Setting and Action Planning linked with the Performance Management that we need to achieve real success.**'

What a contrast to the scene Max had shown me earlier, 28 years in my past when my failure had been dismal. Now I could see that I was going to be a success!

'Max this is great, you have cheered me up, but tell me where did I learn all this stuff?'

'Just here and now,' said Max.

'I learned it from my own future?'

'Yes.'

'That can't be right Max. Where did it come from in the first place?'

'From here.'

'No Max that's cheating and anyway it doesn't make sense.'

'Cheating' said Max 'How is it cheating?'

'I'm getting knowledge from the future to take back and use in the present, making myself look cleverer than I am.'

'It doesn't matter where you get it from, where do you think half of the great inventions came from?'

'You can't be serious Max.' We were back outside the building now watching the pods silently moving in all directions without ever hitting each other.

'Can't I?' replied Max as he fired up the bike's engine and put down his visor. 'Hold on,' came his voice through the helmet intercom again, 'we're moving on pardner!'

Learning Questions

1. What was the cause of Mel's stress at work?
2. What important changes did Marion make?
3. What were the two types of standard that she felt were important?
4. What was the focus of Martin's attention?
5. What tool did he use to gain a picture of where improvement was needed?
6. What actions did Margaret take to improve performance?

Learning Summary – Managing Performance

Managing Performance is about managing the behaviour of people.

A manager must first be clear on what he/she expects and communicate those expectations effectively to team members.

A successful approach is to create a list of tasks that a team member must complete in order to do a good job. Then agree acceptable standards for both quantity and quality of activity with the team member.

Performance against those standards can and must be measured through an appropriate level of monitoring.

When a team member is falling short of standards it is

the manager's role to ensure that the team member develops the skills and motivation to correct the short fall.

All team members need performance managing: even the best will underperform if left alone.

Goal Setting and Action Planning, coupled with effective Performance Management, are an essential set of management and leadership tools.

44

IN CONTROL
(PERFORMANCE AND
PROGRESS)

Part 1

'No.'

'Why not?'

'Because.'

'That's not an answer Max.'

Silence.

'Max, come on it's only fair; you've had a go, now it's my turn. Anyhow, we can't crash into anything can we? We just go straight through things.'

'Yes, but I hate going through moving things, it makes me feel ill.'

'I promise not to go through any moving things.'

Silence.

'Max, you said it would be like old times. We used to share. Max?'

We were sitting on the bike, helmets under our arms. We were nowhere – I mean that, really nowhere! No dark, light, colour, horizon, space, smell – nothing;

just me, Max and the bike. I had asked Max to stop before we arrived at our new destination and here we were – or here we weren't.

'Max, talk to me.'

'Oh alright.' Max turned to look at me. 'But don't drive through any people, I hate that, it goes all red and clammy. And no moving things – that's why I stopped at those traffic lights back there.'

'I promise. So can we go now?'

'Yes.'

'Where are we, anyway?'

'In the space between thoughts.'

'I just wish I hadn't asked that question.'

I climbed off the bike allowing Max to move to the pillion position. Back on the bike with Max behind me I was immediately engaged with various dials and displays that I hadn't previously noticed. I had ridden a bike before but seen nothing that resembled this collection. One little rectangle of light caught my attention where fluorescent purple letters spelled 'Flo'.

'What do I do with this lot, Max?' I asked, as we both put our helmets back on. 'Just start her up and use the throttle, everything else is set to take us the rest of the way.'

'And what is this that says Flo?'

'It's a FriendNav.'

'Which does what?'

'Finds your friends; I put your details in when we started and now it automatically lists your friends. Turn that dial next to the readout.'

I turned the little dial and the name on the readout changed to Mel, then as I kept turning other names appeared and were replaced.

'Hey Max, she's not a friend.' I had stopped on one name.'She doesn't like me.'

'You've got that wrong if she's on the list.'

'And there are a couple of my friends missing.'

'The list is never wrong, I'd think again about your missing 'friends'.'

'Can I get one of these to take home Max?'

'Sorry bud, you will have to wait 10 years before someone invents one.'

'Hey you're on the list Max, but I suppose you know that already.'

'Can we go now?' asked Max

I turned the dial until it read 'Flo' again. At least this time I knew who we were going to see. At last I had a feeling of being back in control of things. But I had a feeling that this feeling wouldn't last for long, feelings being what they are and all that.

Part 2

I expected a bump but got a gentle bounce. We had arrived and my eyes searched for something on which to focus. There came a second and third bounce and then more giving a sensation rather like the rise and fall of an old-fashioned carousel.

Blue sky was the first thing to replace the grey nothing and then a horizon above blue sea. A bright sun was high in the sky and my eyes drawn upwards discovered birds wheeling and squawking. They were sea gulls, we were at the seaside; my spirits rose immediately, like those of any townie at the novelty of an ocean.

We bounced again and I looked down. That's when I shouted 'Max'. In fact I think I shouted his name several times in panic.

'Calm down,' crackled Max's voice through the helmet radio, 'you made a good entrance.'

'Max, we're on water, we're on the sea.' I was looking around for land and there was none, we really were at sea.

'It's ok,' soothed Max, 'we're riding just above the surface, we can do that.'

'We're not going to sink?'

'No, and even if we did we would come to no harm. Remember we're just passing through. We don't touch anything and nothing from here can touch us.'

I recalled my hand passing through Mel and the way we had driven impact-free through walls and doors. I relaxed and looking down again saw that we were indeed riding about two metres above the surface of the water.

'Why are we here, Max?'

'Look to your right,' came the reply.

I did and saw a single ship in the distance.

'We lost some accuracy when we stopped and changed places,' said Max. 'No matter. Just ride across to her and let the FriendNav take control.'

'Ok,' I replied, and turned the bike to face the distant ship. Opening the throttle I felt power surging through the machine as we began to race across the water. I opened her up and we flew, and it felt great. I zig-zagged the bike and, knowing we could not hurt ourselves, got bolder with the turns dipping us to the side as I had seen racing bikes do. Max whooped behind me and shouted me on; we were having fun just like we always had done all those years ago. There was no spray hitting us, although I saw it fly up and - realising it was passing right through us - gave me the idea. We were closing on the ship fast and with about 100 metres to go I took firm hold of the handlebars and drove the bike straight down into the water.

Sound deadened instantly. The bike's roar became a hum, there was a bubbling in my ears, but she didn't falter diving downward, the water around us first light blue, then darker. Our headlight came on automatically and there were fish.

'Oh smart,' said Max

'Not a problem is it?' I asked.

'No just don't fall off. It will take ages to find you again down here.'

Frankly I soon tired of those endless and darkening waters and reaching to the FriendNav that still glowed the name Flo I pushed the auto button as Max had shown me and relaxed my grip on the handlebars. Now I felt like I was on a fairground ride. I heard Max groan.

The bike took a loop moving itself from a downward to an upward trajectory, getting faster and faster. The water quickly got lighter and we saw the surface coming before we got to it, a floaty bright thing above us, and whoosh we were out. I gasped as I saw the huge ship soaring above us. We plunged straight at the cold metal of the hull.

'Ohh wohhhhh,' that was Max. I doubt that anything I may have said was more intelligible.

We flew through the hull and then all I can recall is a blur of images as if someone had set a display of photographs to run at impossible speed – boxes, walls, floors, pipes, people, food, clothes, machines, something red and clammy, 'Sorry Max', engines, water. The bike flew upwards in a direct 'as the crow flies' type straight line towards our target. No subtlety, just speed and efficiency until at last we stopped.

There was a silence before Max spoke, and for once his composed drawl was disturbed. This was a rather rattled Max who said 'Never again buddy'.

I smiled, learning to be reckless again after all this time had been fun. Now, why were we here?

Part 3

'Typical management, tell us nothing and expect everything.'

A man and a woman, both in identical blue overalls, were talking conspiratorially.

'Who does he think he is?' she replied. 'A right little Napoleon with his stupid speeches; 'commitment', ' team work' – does he think we were born yesterday?' She was mimicking someone, changing her voice to a childish sing-song as she emphasised the words she disliked. 'He spouts this nonsense but he's only interested in making his wage and getting promoted.'

'He doesn't like me anyway, ever since that time I refused to work late. I can tell from the way he looks at me.'

'Typical management, just like you said. This new system is just to make him look good, it won't make any difference.'

'And this training they want to give us, what's that all about? Last place I worked they got people on training to figure out who they were going to sack.'

'Really?'

'Yes, no question; they looked at who wasn't doing so well with it and guess who went when the redundancies came?'

'The little conniving weasel, I've never liked him.'

'You should have had his job anyway, you've been working on these cruising ships for years.'

'I know, but that's management for you. Claim you haven't been on the right course and give the job to one of their own.'

Max tapped my arm, 'Come on, I think we got the picture here,' and since he had now taken the riding position, he moved us forward gracefully gliding through a couple of walls until we found ourselves listening to another conversation.

'They're a poisonous bunch, Flo, impossible to handle, always gossiping, and complaining that they've been hard done by. None of them will take responsibility; they always expect me to solve their problems for them. I wouldn't mind if they were really good at their jobs, but none of them are outstanding. They're slow and sometimes downright incompetent, but never anything serious enough to justify getting rid of them. My boss employed most of them before I got the job, he doesn't think we would get any better if we recruited again. It's a mess, I wish I had your people, they seem to have such a great attitude.'

'They have but don't expect me to say I'm lucky.'

'No, I didn't mean …'

'It takes careful work to get people co-operating and motivated.'

I was happy to see Flo. She had always been a good friend, reliable, open, honest. Someone you could talk to. She and I talked together a lot back in the old days when we shared the flat. She had the ability to make you feel relaxed and so you would open up to her, but she was never one to back off telling you something you didn't want to hear. Today she sounded as strong and confident as ever and I could see the young man talking to her had a respect for her. In contrast he seemed lacking in confidence and it became clear that he was the manager, the 'little Napoleon' that the people we had just overheard had been talking about.

'Flo I need some help,' he blurted out, the bravado vanishing. 'I can't control these people.'

'Is it the first time?' Flo asked.

'What do you mean?'

'Is this the first time you've had difficulty with people you manage?'

After a pause he answered, 'No, it isn't.'

'Then let's cover some basics and see what's wrong.'

'They don't like me.'

'They don't respect you is probably more accurate.'

The other manager looked hurt and quietly replied, 'Yes you are right, they don't.'

'But that's not the problem,' said Flo, 'that's the result of the problem. We need to find out what's causing this lack of respect. Do you give them direction?'

'Yes, of course. I make clear plans, goals and targets. They all know what's expected.'

'And how do you ensure performance?'

'I manage it. We have standards for quantity and

quality, agreed by everyone, and I check them.'

'So where is the problem?'

'It seems however many goals, standards and processes I have in place, we always need more. There's always something that falls outside a process and we have to endlessly add new parts to try and cover all possibilities, and then often what we have agreed just doesn't work or doesn't get done. But since none of them seem to care, problems mount up and we spend much time rushing around sorting things out.'

'It sounds to me as if they don't want your performance management processes to work, or they don't care whether they work or not.'

'I wouldn't disagree with that. They think it's us and them, management and workers, and I guess they are right. Why should they care?'

'But let me remind you of your earlier comment about my people and their attitude. You were right, they are positive and they care about the quality of the job they deliver. We have performance management processes in place and they work.'

'Well I don't understand; why can't I get that from my people?'

'Because mine want them to work and yours don't care. **If your people don't want your performance management to work, it never will,** not fully. And if your management of performance is not first rate you can never achieve a high performing team. Instead your performance management systems and processes will be a source of stress and frustration.' She paused and let her message sink in, then adding, 'Do you talk to them?'

'Of course I talk to them.' His voice displayed irritation.

'About what?'

'About the job, about the issues that arise every day, we talk all the time.' His tone was rising. But Flo's was not, she remained her steady relentless self. I smiled recalling a few grillings that she had given me in the past (or was it the future? Not sure that I knew anymore!) 'About the job?' she probed.

'Yes, that's what I just said.'

'And what about them, do you talk about them?'

'I don't get what you mean.'

'Do you talk to them about themselves and their development, about how they are doing, about how they can move their skills and abilities forward? Do you talk about them as people?'

'Of course,' but he didn't sound confident.

'How much do you know about them? Their home lives, families and interests, strengths and weaknesses, their ambitions?'

'I'm their manager not their social worker, Flo.'

'You've done your Hidden Treasure course about Leadership, you know what team members need from their leader.'

'It was a long time ago.'

'Well forget it at your peril, and that is part of your problem. If you don't fulfil those needs their respect will fall away. It sounds as if you focus on Task Needs and ignore Individual Needs. You don't need to be a social worker, but you do need to be a smart manager if you want respect and co-operation from your people.'

'I do complete an annual appraisal.'

'And is that a positive experience?

'No. I fill in that damned form and send it to HR. I hate it and so do the team, it just gives them an excuse to complain and ask for more money and me a reason to get in a bad mood.'

'So do you still want my help?'

'Yes, of course.'

'It didn't sound like it a few moments ago.'

He managed an apologetic grin, seemed to relax and regain his composure. 'No I'm sorry. This whole thing has me really stressed. I would value your advice.'

'Ok but don't waste my time, if I give you advice I expect you to use it, put it into practice. You have to do things differently if you want a different result. Agreed?'

I cringed at her steamroller style, but reflected that it's amazing what you can get away with when you have the respect of the other person.

'Yes Flo.'

'No taking half my advice, the half that suits you. You need to start behaving differently, and frankly that takes courage.'

'Ok, I give in. Please, tell me what I can do.'

'Not now,' smiled Flo changing the tone and pace of the conversation for something a little smoother, 'I have a challenge I need to attend to in the bridal suite.'

'Problem?'

'They're lottery winners and newly weds, loads of money and never had it before; it's all a bit challenging. They want everything, want it now and treat my staff like slaves not people, not the way to get the best from them is it? Never mind, we'll handle it; in the meantime please think about what we have said. **If you don't talk with your people about their performance and development** you can be sure they will assume you **lack interest in them,** they will feel **uncertainty about their own progress, suspicion about your**

motivations and **frustration over concerns not discussed.** This is a two way problem because you will feel **suspicious of their motivations,** you will **misunderstand reasons for their underperformance and you will feel a lack of support from them.**

The cabin door opened and a member of Flo's team appeared. 'We've sorted it,' she said, 'a couple of the team dealt with it straight away and the happy couple are happy again.'

'Great,' replied Flo with a smile, 'where would I be without you?'

'No problem,' replied the friendly face and closed the door as she left.

Flo turned again. 'I can help, let's meet on the main deck this afternoon and I will have time to give you some advice.'

Part 4

Wispy clouds tickled the face of a laughing sun in an otherwise blue, blue sky.

Squinting in the sunlight I held a hand up to shield my eyes as I breathed in salty air and admired the luxuriant gardens. They truly were a surprise, luscious green grass, boldly coloured flower beds, and trees; extraordinary on the deck of a ship! But what a ship. I couldn't see the sea behind us it was obscured by trees while in front was eventually a view of the sea, beyond a series of high fenced tennis courts. Looking to what I assumed was forrard seemed a great distance in which rose buildings, funnels and flags, until there must have been a prow which was quite out of sight. And in the opposite direction the stern was lost beyond a busy market place teeming with stalls and shoppers. The young manager we had seen earlier was sitting on a bench.

We had, according to Max, arrived a few minutes early because I must have touched some dial or other when I was riding the bike; it had to be my fault of course.

'Ever heard of a no blame culture, Max?' I enquired.

'No,' he replied, 'Where's the fun if you can't blame anyone?'

'It's about assuming no intent to get it wrong and seeking a way to better times rather than dwelling on who done it,' I persisted.

'Mmmm. Doesn't get round the fact that it's your fault, does it?'

I decided to leave that one for another occasion. 'We're only a few minutes early you said.'

'Yes.'

'Then tell me about this ship, Max. It's huge.'

'It's a residential cruiser, half tourist half residence.'

'People live on it?'

'Yes, rising sea levels mean less land and more sea, we are seven years ahead of your home time and you know there was a real problem developing back then.'

'People live on here all the time?'

'They will have sold up on land, or in some cases lost all on land and bought residence on board a ship like this. In ten years time the seas will be full of them. There are huge teams of workers on them just to keep the whole thing going, they're like floating towns. Get one like this based in the Mediterranean and it's a good investment. Can't afford that, then you get the North Sea.'

Just then Flo arrived up a stairway that gave onto the lawn and looked appreciatively up at the sky and sun. Putting on a pair of sunglasses slipped from an inside pocket of her jacket, she walked across to the bench.

'Beautiful day,' she said, sitting on the bench. She stretched her legs and held her arms out in the warming rays. A policeman walked past nodding to them both, a young couple passed in the opposite direction. 'It's quite outrageous of you to think that it won't change things,' we heard as they passed.

'Isn't it great?' replied the manager to Flo, 'Just the kind of day I imagined when I signed up for this ship. Help me get my stress levels down, Flo, and I can start enjoying it a bit more!'

'I've considered your challenge,' began Flo, 'and it's clear that what's missing is positive motivation. Your people don't want your team to work; they don't want your processes to work. Here you have a problem; it's in almost everyone's nature to want to do a good job because essentially that's a way that we gain satisfaction and a sense of purpose in life. When the culture of an organisation, or its people's perception of that culture, prevents them from gaining that satisfaction then they must find purpose in another way, and that way will often be in becoming judgemental of the organisation and its leaders. They gain their self-esteem from a feeling of holding the moral high ground, being right while others are wrong. This will show itself in people being critical of you and uncooperative, just the situation you have.'

'Just the situation.' repeated the young manager. 'They don't cooperate. When my back is turned, I can never be sure that they are carrying out my instructions. We spend large amounts of time dealing with people issues amongst the team rather than getting on with the job. They're always back biting amongst each other or forming small groups to single out one of the team for criticism. It is ceaseless and makes my job hell.'

'So you have to address the reason for the problem. You must lead them to a position where they gain satisfaction and a sense of purpose from the job. You need them to reverse their negative mind frame and if you can do this they will turn positive thoughts toward the team, to you and to the tasks that you must complete as a team'.

'I suppose I can understand that Flo, because I have similar feelings at times toward our boss.'

'And does he ever talk with you about your development?'

'Ha, ha! He occasionally talks to me about my impending dismissal if I don't sort my team's performance out. Come on Flo, I buy the explanation, now what's the solution?'

'Your 'solution', as you put it, will involve careful consideration of how you are fulfilling the group needs of your team through your leadership and how you are satisfying the requirements of team building. You should refresh yourself on your Hidden Treasure principles. One major change that will help you is the introduction of occasional meetings with each individual to discuss their progress in the team.'

'Flo I told you earlier that I talk with them all the time.'

'Yes about aspects of the job, about today's problem, about the latest backbiting around another team member; that's not the kind of discussion I mean. I want you to sit down with them **one to one**, perhaps once every three months or so and talk to them about the most important subject in the world to them: themselves! I want you to discuss **how they feel their job is going** and tell them **how you think they are doing**, talk about **how they are developing** and **how they can develop**, and then talk about **what you and they can do to make it happen**. Have you ever done that before?'

'No I can't say I have, and neither can I say any boss has ever done that with me.'

'How would you feel if your boss did do that with you? Spent a little time talking about **you** with the obvious aim of helping you grow and develop?'

'I would be flattered and I suppose encouraged. I don't think my boss is in the slightest bit interested in me as a person or in my development.'

'Why do you think that?'

'Ok, you've got me. Yes the answer is because he has never talked to me about it, so I assume he has no interest.'

'Do you know for sure?'

'No, of course not.'

'Have I made my point?'

'Yes but perhaps it's not that easy. Frankly I think I would feel a bit awkward about a conversation like that. I hate doing annual appraisals, can't wait to get them out of the way. The idea of sitting down and having a personal conversation like that especially with some of my more difficult team members is not attractive.'

'No, you don't feel confident about doing it, which means you may well appear nervous or as if you don't really care but are going through the motions. That's probably what happens when you conduct your annual appraisal meetings.'

'I think you're right Flo, that's just how I feel and those meetings are almost all uncomfortable and on many occasions lead to friction.'

'Then we must help you be more confident in handling these meetings, both the annual reviews and interim discussions'.

'You are suggesting I do more appraisals?' His voice rose in dismay.

'Not quite. I want you to hold an annual review, you can call it an appraisal if you want, with each of your staff members at which you review their development for the last year and agree objectives for the year ahead. Then I want you to hold some shorter interim meetings to talk about how they are doing and review their objectives if necessary. After all there's no point in agreeing something and then leaving it for 12 months before you check on it.'

'That's a big ask, Flo, when I hate the meetings anyway.'

'Yes but that's why we need to build your skills at handling these meetings, you should come to find them positive experiences. Let's begin with setting them up correctly so that both of you arrive in the right frame of mind. To start with **give at least 24 hours notice**, don't hold these meetings without warning. Why do you think that would be important?'

'I've no idea, you tell me.'

Flo looked sternly at the young manager. 'If you are

not prepared to work at this then I am not going to take up my time helping you.'

'Sorry Flo', he replied. 'I suppose if we give someone notice they have time to think about it.'

'Correct' replied Flo, 'they have time to mentally prepare. After all this is an important meeting for them and people do not usually react well to surprises. Also make sure that if you are holding several of these meetings that you **hold no more than two per day**: more and you will find that you are not giving the focus and concentration that they require. If you try for three at the third your mind will be drifting and your team member will notice and feel slighted. Which is also true if you **cancel** one of these meetings without immediately arranging another date; this is a meeting with an agenda of just one thing, them. These will be amongst the most important meetings they ever have, so treat them thoughtfully because if you treat them carelessly the insult is great.'

'Ok I can see that,' said the young manager.

'Hold them on **neutral ground,**' continued Flo,' **prepare the room** and make sure you will have **no interruptions**.'

'What do you mean by neutral ground?' He had produced a notebook and was scribbling furiously as she spoke.

'I mean somewhere that is neither your territory nor theirs.'

'You mean not in my office?'

'Ideally not, but equally not in their workspace, and if you have to use your own office then move your chair to the other side of your desk and sit with the other person rather than face each other across your desk.'

'That would make a real difference?'

'Certainly, it would create a more open and friendly feel for your meeting, whereas across a desk would signal confrontation leading to a more defensive approach from the other person and setting you both up to head for conflict.'

'I've got that, and what do you mean by prepare the room?'

'Make sure it's not messy, make sure any desk space is clear, make it look as if you have prepared for this meeting and taken it seriously. The worst scene here would be you having this meeting in your own office, across your own desk which is covered in papers and files, with open filing cabinets and other distractions around you. This gives out the message that you have not taken this meeting seriously, that it is an interruption for you. You can be sure that the other person will pick up on this and as a result your meeting will not go well.'

'I'd never considered any of this before, and it's all before we have even begun to talk! But it makes sense.'

'It certainly does. What I'm telling you is the most important thing that I suspect I am doing and you are not. You admired the attitude of my people earlier and in my view they are like that because I put them in a situation where they respond positively and these 'progress meetings' as I call them are a significant key to making this happen'.

Flo stood up and stretched. Come on let's walk; I need some exercise. The other stood and disconcertingly Flo turned and walked straight through Max. 'Nooo' he groaned and I stepped aside to avoid her colleague as they headed through the trees behind us and towards a small lake that came into view. Max and I followed, me trying to absorb the flood of information from Flo and Max still grumbling about being walked through.

Part 5

The two were walking around the edge of a small lake. The only birds to be seen were seagulls, and ahead as we moved clear of the trees the sea appeared on the other side of the huge ship.

'We have discussed how to prepare for a 'progress meeting' now we need to think about how to conduct one,' said Flo, 'if you don't enjoy your appraisal discussions then you need to think hard about how you conduct these meetings. **Get the other person to talk early in the discussion; ask before you tell**, **don't talk too much** and **use open-ended questions**. Those are the ones that cannot be answered with a yes or no, they are the 'how', 'why' or 'what' questions, ideal for getting someone to speak. Remember everything you have learned about **assertive communication** and how your communication will affect their attitude. Use **assertive and positive non-verbal communication along with assertive words**. That means **face them full on, use good eye contact, have a smile on your face and find a relaxed way to show the palm of at least one of your hands** – it will make a positive difference to how they think and respond. **Listen carefully**, **watch their non-verbal** communication. Are they relaxed or nervous? Does the situation improve as you keep talking? In other words, be focussed on the other person.'

'I never imagined there would be so much to remember.' Once again he had his notebook and pen in hand.

'With practise it becomes second nature,' smiled Flo, 'but practise is the key, you need to start doing this with your people and keep it up.'

'You've talked about the style but what about the content?'

'**Follow a simple structure of prepared questions;** this will help you keep on track when the conversation ranges around other things that your team member may introduce, and will allow you to be flexible enough to discuss other issues that they may raise without losing your own direction. **Don't duck conflict**, confront it, and **don't miss opportunities for praise and positive comment. Focus on the future,** don't dwell on past incidents. You will of course need to refer to what has happened, but this discussion is about this person's development in the future and that is what you should be concentrating on. **Consider their typical performance, not the highs and lows;** you want to help them lift their day-to-day performance to make a real difference.'

'I see that; and is there anything that I should avoid doing?'

'Yes, **don't talk about salary or disciplinary matters**, both are subjects for quite separate discussions. If you touch on either of these there is a strong chance that they will dominate the conversation and thinking which will divert you from your intended subject.'

Flo paused as he made his notes. When he stopped he asked 'Is that it Flo?'

'Not quite. You must make sure that this discussion will lead to some action; there is no point in discussing an individual's progress and development, then allowing nothing to happen. You should be seeking to **agree some actions** to follow the meeting, and to make sure they occur you should **write them down**, **let the other person have a copy** and, if necessary, schedule activity into your diary and schedule a **follow up** when you will check that they are doing what they have committed to do. People can be lazy even about their own development; a reminder from you could make the difference between nothing happening between your meetings and an individual making real progress. **Set some measurable objectives** and **ask the team member to keep track of their performance and learning.** At the end of the meeting you should **summarise what has been agreed**, and check that they accept that your summary is accurate.' She stopped walking and gazed out to sea; evidently her advice was complete.

He finished his writing and, slipping the notebook back into his pocket, he grinned. 'Thanks Flo, this is an aspect of managing people that I have never considered, yet as you point it out I can see what a difference it could make. I must tell you that I'm nervous about it. I have some strong characters amongst my team and they seem fairly well set in their attitude towards me.'

'There will only be a problem if you let there be,' replied Flo. Now I smiled at the way she never let anyone off the hook. 'If you don't do it,' she continued, 'then your situation will only get worse. If you start to do this and keep it up you will see a gradual change. You can't expect an instant turn around but you can expect small signs of improvement and for some individuals to respond quicker than others. You should also expect to feel unsure and nervous because you are trying something different. If you are really working at it then I am happy to talk with you again and give you any advice that I am able to. As you start to win some supporters amongst the team then others will begin to follow until those who hold out the longest will begin to find themselves isolated in their opposition to you. You must also remember to review your whole leadership style. Building better respect and understanding with your team members in this way must be complemented by other good leadership skills. Remember to fulfil their Task, Team and Individual needs, remember to use Assertive Communication, Coach your people, use Delegation to create Motivation and Build a Team, make sure all of those Hidden Treasure skills are in use.'

'I will.'

'Good,' replied Flo, 'because if you don't we've just been wasting our time.'

'I promise I will and I appreciate your help.'

'Ok' she said smiling again, 'time for me to get back to work. Keep me up to date, let me know how you are doing.' And with that Flo walked off toward a covered stairway and disappeared back down into the ship. The young manager found another bench and taking the notebook back out of his pocket began to read what he had written.

'Time to go,' said Max, 'that's our lesson complete.' I looked up at the blue sky and bright sun and, noticing that I could not feel the warmth, experienced a desire to go home. 'Is our journey finished, Max?'

'Not yet,' he answered. 'There are two more experiences that I think will help you. You still wanna come along?'

'Of course I do, Max. I'm learning too much to stop now. I guess my real world will have to wait a little longer.' Together we walked back along the path to where the black motorbike, only visible to ourselves, waited at the point we had first arrived on this vast deck. Sitting again on the back of the bike I took one last look around at sea and sky. Max fired up the engine and, I think in a small act of revenge for my earlier adventure in control of the bike, let the throttle full out and hurtled at speed through mesh fences and across tennis courts toward the side of the ship which we did not reach because of the grey cloud that appeared in front of us and into which we rode.

Learning Questions

1. Why were the young manager's performance management methods not working?
2. What did Flo say would happen if you don't talk to team members about their performance and development?
3. How do you get the other person talking at a review meeting?
4. What should you do at the end of a review meeting?
5, What should you do after a review meeting?

Learning Summary – Performance and Progress

If your team members don't want your performance management systems to work then they will never work to best effect.

To maintain interest and motivation a manager must talk regularly with team members about their performance and development.

To be effective with these discussions the manager should:

- Give at least 24 hours notice
- Hold the meeting on neutral ground without interruptions
- Ensure the other person does plenty of talking

- Communicate positively and assertively
- Follow a simple structure of prepared questions
- Agree some actions and write them down
- Set some measurable objectives and keep track of progress toward them

OPEN THE BOX (MANAGING CHANGE)

Part 1

Strings zinged to a crescendo, ripping alongside a rampaging brass section and thundering drums. This was music to excite and we were excited. I held on to Max so hard my fingers ached and my eyes watered as I peered around him receiving a blast of air in my face. The two of us were once again on the back of Excellence who was galloping mightily.

'Yeehaaa!' shouted Max.

I didn't shout anything.

Max was urging Ex on, throwing the reigns and kicking his heels.

'Gotta get clear of those injuns' yelled Max, his cowboy drawl back at full strength. I dared a small downward flick of my eyes and recognised that we were both back in cowboy clothes.

The music was driving the scene at a hysterical pace, the drumming like horses' hooves, the strings a prairie fire roaring through a tune I almost recognised, the brass big and bold.

'Move 'em on, head 'em up' yelled Max.

'Max what are you talking about?'

'Count 'em out, ride 'em in.'

'Max you're talking nonsense.' Ex still galloped, there was sweat on his broad flanks, the music swelled. I looked behind us for 'injuns', there were none. 'Max there are no injuns'.

'Goddamit, don't try to understand 'em, just rope and throw and brand 'em.'

'Max those are the lyrics to Rawhide.'

'Pardner?'

'And that accent Max, I meant to ask you earlier, it doesn't sound completely convincing.'

Ex was slowing, as was the music.

'Hey buddy you used to like old rollin, rollin, rollin.'

'Max we've just been on board a ship and you didn't talk like this at all.'

Ex cantered to a stop and so did the music. Max sat straight, held the reigns loose and rested his hands on the front of the saddle. Without turning he said 'You don't like being a cowboy anymore?'

'I didn't say that Max, I was just curious as to whether that was your real accent.'

'*Of course it's not his real accent*' said a third cultured voice.

I span my head seeking the new speaker.

'No he's right,' said Max, now with a neutral enunciation, 'but that's how we talk when we're having a cowboy adventure.'

'When we used to have cowboy adventures,' I corrected.

'Oh yes' he replied. 'I keep forgetting you're a

grown up now. Is that fun?'

'It's …' I paused to consider my reply, 'it's different, Max, I'm sorry I didn't mean to upset you.'

'*He's not upset, just disappointed.*'

'Who is that?' I asked

'It's Ex' Max was turning to look at me now. 'You alright?'

My eyes must have widened as I looked past Max to Ex's head. 'Ex is talking?'

'No he doesn't talk he just sometimes lets you know what he's thinking. Oh and he sometimes plays music when he's having fun.'

'*Yes I have always liked a good game of cowboys and injuns.*'

'Sorry guys, looks like I've spoilt it. It's just a long time since I've played like that.'

'Well never mind' said Max brightening, 'we've got another surprise for you. Recognise where we are?'

I began to take in my surroundings. 'Since we are back on Ex does this mean we are in my past?'

'Well done. You're getting the hang of this at last.'

'I know this place, only too well. This was where I worked about six or seven years ago.'

'Seven,' confirmed Max.

'It wasn't particularly good for me. Is this going to be embarrassing Max, are we going to see me getting it horribly wrong again?'

I'm sure Ex sniggered as Max confirmed that indeed we were going to begin our next adventure by observing my failure. Lifting the reigns he urged Ex into a sedate trot, as I prepared to be humiliated.

Part 2

'It's the bored room.'

'He's in one of *those* moods ignore him. You don't hear a thing for months and then he suddenly tunes in to you,' said Max.

We were outside a closed door bearing a sign that read 'Board Room'.

'I don't think my meetings were that bad Ex,' I replied. 'In fact I prided myself on bringing some energy and enthusiasm to my management meetings.'

'Which is what we've come to see; shall we proceed?' Max had dropped the cowboy drawl and was talking with no discernable accent in a quiet but business like manner.

'Max I rather liked the cowboy talk.'

'Ha!'

'No I'm sure you were right, this is serious, no room for horseplay ...' replied Max.

'Nice one Max.'

'... we are on adult, grown up business, we will behave professionally. See?' Max raised his hands to shoulder height and pointed his fingers back at himself, which is when I noticed that his cowboy outfit had been replaced by a smart grey business suit, white shirt and tasteful tie. I was wearing the same and felt a pang of disappointment; there had been something daring and stylish about the silver spurs and six shooters.

'Yes, don't you both look wonderfully dull; can we get on with this now?'

Max, clearly practised at ignoring Ex, said 'Let's go and have a look at how you were getting along seven years ago,' and needing no further urging, Ex transported us through the wall and into the boardroom.

Inside the familiar room I saw myself, seven years the younger and fresh faced. 'I've still got that suit Max.'

'Fascinating, I don't think I'd own up to that, but then whoever saw a horse wearing a suit?'

Part 3

The younger me was animated. It took me a while to remember this meeting but slowly it came back as I watched myself addressing the team of six that had been my sales department. I was presenting an idea for changing the way we delivered to our customers, and slowly I remembered. I had read something in a newspaper over the preceding weekend that had sparked an idea; it was about how another organisation had made major improvements by considering the full customer experience as part of the sales process. The idea was that as sales people we usually moved on to the next customer after concluding the sales agreement and as a result the customer experience that followed was often poor. This put some people off coming back to us again and from recommending us to friends; the idea was to change this for the better by making delivery part of the sales process with involvement from the sales team. We were to create a detailed process for after the sale, as detailed as we had for getting the sale in the first place. What I also recalled was that in fact this idea never worked, and after a few weeks we reverted to the original way of doing things.

But the meeting looked good. My enthusiasm was apparent, some of the team were smiling, one of them was getting involved and making suggestions, he looked really sold on the idea. As I concluded my presentation there were smiles and nodding heads around the room.

'Shame it just wasn't a workable idea, Max. I remember this; it got a really good response from the team. We tried to get a new system going but there just weren't enough hours in the day to make it happen. You have to give new things a try, but they don't always work out; that's business.'

'So why do you think I brought you back to this meeting?' asked Max.

'I have no idea, I can't remember what else we talked about, is there more to come?'

'No we've seen the important bit and now I want to show you what happened after the meeting.'

Part 4

We were in a corridor following two of the team.

'What do you think?' asked the first.

'No chance, it'll never work,' replied the second.

'But you can't say that. We don't want to look like we're not backing the idea.'

'No of course not, but it would mean so much more work.'

'We're going to have to do something.'

'Just go through the motions. We'll soon move on to the next bright idea and forget about it.'

'They never think these things through; imagine the effect it would have on the other teams. They would all have to change processes as well, it would be a nightmare.'

'I told you just go through the motions for a few days, it'll soon go away.'

'Yes and we spent a lot of time getting this sales process right and now he's saying it's not good enough'.

'We're too busy anyhow.'

Ex moved us on and now we were in the car park; the team member who had got more involved and made suggestions in the meeting was with one of the others.

'You seemed pretty keen on that new idea.'

'Yes I'm sure it could make a real difference.'

'Really?'

'Yes but the problem is you can't introduce these things too quickly if you want them to work. We need a few months to get a good plan together, work out just how to make it work.'

'So we don't need to bother right now?'

'No, too busy aren't we? The boss will come up with a plan and we can hold a couple of meetings to discuss it.'

'So we don't need to actually do anything right now?'

'Well it's the last week of the month isn't it, have you got any time right now?'

'No chance.'

'It's a good idea though, a really good idea.'

Now I was beginning to feel embarrassed and following close on the heels of embarrassment came anger. 'Max, they never even tried'.

'No. So was it a good idea or a bad one?'

'I don't know. I'll never know.'

'And what about the other ideas that never worked

for your team? Remember the plan to change the rosta system to give longer opening hours that failed?'

'Yes, and I remember when we tried to change the bonus scheme, it was a total disaster. In fact now you make me think about it, changing things was always hard work. But it didn't always fail Max, I can think of plenty of changes we made work. After all we had to change every time we got a new product.'

'Yes those changes were inevitable, but did they happen smoothly?'

'What do you mean?'

'Did they happen quickly and with minimum fuss?'

'I suppose not as quickly as I would have liked, but then you're dealing with human nature aren't you? You must expect change to be a difficult thing.'

'And change is something you are faced with all the time.'

'I suppose it is. In this job,' I pointed back at the building, 'there was a new product range twice a year. The way our customers behaved definitely changed and we had to react to that; there was staff turnover so we had new faces, other departments made changes which meant we had to change something, our competitors changed. I remember when a competitor introduced a 24-hour service and it wasn't long before we had to do the same.'

'So you were constantly dealing with change?'

'I guess I was, although I had never thought about it in this way before.'

'So whether your team were good or bad at dealing with change became important to you.'

'I see your point. Making change happen was a major pressure on me.'

'And on your team,'

'Yes I suppose it was, and certainly a major source of stress for me.'

'And for your team.'

'So what's your point here, Max?'

'My point is that you weren't very good at handling change as the team leader.'

'Wasn't I?'

'No just look at what happened in that meeting.'

'I presented my idea clearly and with commitment and enthusiasm. There's no way they didn't understand it, I thought carefully about how to explain it. I used a flipchart to show the idea visually.'

'So why didn't they grab it and try to make it happen?'

'They were lazy?'

'No, when you introduce change there is more to it than getting people to understand your idea. If you want your people to embrace a change you must help them adapt mentally to it and if you don't they will resist. Most of us are the same, we don't like change, especially when it comes as a surprise.'

'Ok so are you going to show me how it could be done better?'

'Yes, can you remember what happened over the weekend before that meeting?'

'Seven years ago, you must be joking.'

'Well think about the idea you had, where did it come from?'

'From reading the Sunday paper; ah yes and discussing it with Tom. We were still sharing a flat, he was a real bright spark and a really unusual character. I remember now we had a long discussion about it, got me fired up and that's how I came into work on Monday with this idea.'

'Shall we see how Tom introduced a new idea?'

'He did it differently to me?'

'He did.'

'The sly devil he never told me.'

'Maybe he thought you were too boring old Grey Suit.'

'Hey, not so much of the old.'

'Come on,' said Max 'let's move on'. And once more we set off, Ex again at a controlled trot, Max and I in our smart grey suits. I had to admit that it wasn't anything like as exciting as the way we had arrived.

Part 5

The air was damp and warm and there was a smell that I couldn't place – not unpleasant. The noise wasn't calamitous; it was a mix of chug and swish. We were standing in front of a great roll of brown paper, almost 6 metres in diameter that was being fed slowly along runners and between rollers and away from us to more machinery.

'What do they do here Max?'

'Make cardboard and turn it into packaging.'

'And this is where Tom worked?'

'Yes'

'They make cardboard boxes!'

'Yes'

'He told me he managed a casino.'

'A lively imagination at work.'

'Oh yes Tom often let his imagination run riot. By

the way where is everybody?' I realised there were no people, just machinery.

And then just one person appeared.

'Oh my goodness, is this meant to be funny Max?'

'Oh sweet irony.'

'Nothing to do with me' said Max 'I can only bring you here, what happens is far beyond my control.'

The figure that had appeared striding across the factory floor was Tom, dressed as a cowboy! Boots, chaps, silver spurs, leather jacket with fringed sleeves and Stetson hat; he had the full outfit. He was making a determined passage along a marked walkway through the machinery and we followed to a pair of double doors marked 'Boxes. Eatery for craftsmen'. Tom placed the palm of a hand on the handle of each door and flung them inwards like a gunslinger making an entrance to a downtown saloon, and as he did an eruption of cheers, shouting and applause was released from within. The large room was full, solving the riddle of the missing factory workers.

As Tom made his way through the room to a small platform in one corner several people clapped him on the back, many were laughing, pointing and cheering, there were wolf whistles. Everyone seemed to be watching Tom apart from two love birds at the back gazing into each other's eyes and she clearly besotted with him, saying nothing more than 'outrageous'. On the platform Tom raised his hands and the room quietened to a good humoured buzz.

'Now you know we did it!' he yelled

And the room yelled back, hands up in the air applauding.

'Don't applaud me, applaud yourselves. **We** did it!'

When the room quietened again Tom continued. He pointed to some posters on the walls. They illustrated three bullet holes, a cowboy with smoking six guns and the slogan 'let's shoot up those targets'.

'Two weeks ago we started the new system. It was very different to the way we have always done it; I know many of you were worried and I want to thank you for your support. It's your ideas that have made this our success. Now I can tell you that we have shot those targets to pieces; production is up 15% already and many of you know that re runs are down as well. We did it!'

Tom took off the Stetson and waved it in the air to another round of cheers and hand-clapping from his audience. 'So a promise is a promise. I wore the hat for the two weeks and now the full outfit on achieving our success. Enjoy your bonus and extra day off, you earned if fair and square. It's an impressive achievement.'

Just then the double doors swung open again. This time it was not a cowboy but a severe looking lady in a tweed suit, who looked disconcerted by the unexpected and lively crowd. All faces turned to look at the new arrival, who addressed Tom across the room with the words, 'The Chairman would like to see you Mr Rose'.

'Now?' replied Tom.

'Yes right away please, she has to leave in 30 minutes and wants to see you before she goes.'

'No time to change?'

'I'm afraid not,' replied the lady in the doorway.

So Tom took his leave of the room, who were given further reason for merriment by the turn of events, and Max and I followed as Tom the cowboy set off to meet the Chairman.

Part 6

'Good morning Mr Rose. Is this your usual mode of dress for the factory floor these days?' The Chairman had raised an eyebrow on Tom's arrival.

'No Ma'am. Today is a special occasion. I can explain'.

'I'm sure you will, and please call me Charlotte,' said the Chairman. 'In fact I think you have rather a lot of explaining to do.'

'I have?' gulped Tom looking worried.

'Yes,' smiled the Chairman. 'I want you to explain this unexpected increase in your production figures.' And then noting Tom's pale face added, 'Don't worry, Tom, you're not in trouble. I am impressed and want to know how you've done it. And if you can persuade me that it has been achieved by all staff dressing as cowboys then I shall order my six guns in the morning!'

The Chairman indicated a seat and looked expectantly at Tom, 'Well?'

Tom sat, 'It's a straightforward answer Ma'a … er Charlotte, we introduced a new system two weeks ago and it's working.'

'I am well aware of that Tom; I do read the management reports.'

'Yes, I didn't mean to suggest …'

'No I'm sure you didn't,' said the Chairman. 'I would like to hear about the new system, but there is more to it than that. Not only have you introduced a new system but you have done it in two weeks, with a workforce that is notoriously hard to change. I am surprised. I expected it to take you several months and then that your chances of success would be limited. I have seen many new ideas die quickly on that factory floor and yet you, young man, appear to have introduced a new system that impacts on every one of those workers and done it in double quick time. How?'

'Oh you're asking about my management of the change.'

'I am. How have you achieved it?'

'Do you mind if I take these guns off, Charlotte? They look good but they're murder to sit down in.'

The Chairman waved her agreement, looking a little impatiently at her watch as Tom unbuckled the belt on which the two holsters were held and laid them on the Chairman's desk. I couldn't quite decide whether this was Tom having a little fun or just being his usual unusual self.

'I saw the change in **two stages**.' Tom began his explanation. 'The first was **the planning stage** and the second **the implementation**. **For planning there were four things** that I made sure were achieved, and I believe all four of them contributed to a reduction in resistance to the change I was trying to bring about.

The first was to **avoid surprises**; many people react negatively when surprised with a change, so I began to sow the seeds of the idea several weeks before any attempt to introduce the change. I got people thinking about how we could change the system for the better, started asking people for their thoughts, and began to mention at meetings that we would have to make some changes to remain competitive.

This meant that when I got to the second thing, which was to **involve people in the planning of the change,** I had already reduced the amount of resistance. Involving people in planning reduces stress, which is exaggerated when people feel out of control. If they play even a small part it allows them to feel that they have some understanding of what is happening. If you tell people nothing or as little a possible they feel powerless and react negatively to that feeling.

Alongside involving people I made sure that **everyone had a shared vision** of what we were aiming to achieve. I tried to ensure that everyone got a clear picture of the planned change, step-by-step, and a clear picture of the desired and expected outcome. A shared vision is essential for team working, just as a clear vision of an objective is essential for individual motivation. For each person to understand the overall goal and the part they played in realising that goal would dictate the enthusiasm and commitment with which they approached the change. Contrast this thinking with keeping people in the dark and hijacking them with a new idea in which they have no input and you can see why this way should reduce resistance to change and the other way would create it.

There is a fourth important element of the planning stage, which is to **minimise the impact of past resentments**. Grievances from the past can hold back someone's ability to accept change. There was some resentment about the previous production manager's attempt to change the bonus structure, which they saw only as a way to reduce their income. This was nothing to do with what we were trying to achieve, but it was nevertheless important to some of the team. My job was to listen, discuss and give reassurance and direction as appropriate. The point is that my actions were not going to re-write history, but the act of simply taking notice and discussing past resentment reduces its power in the mind of those who carry that resentment.

That's how I planned for the change in terms of reducing resistance amongst the team. That takes us to the implementation and a further eight considerations.'

The Chairman had been listening with great interest but now stopped Tom by raising her hand, and said 'Tom this is most interesting. Regrettably I have an engagement and need to leave soon, so let's put the rest of this conversation on hold. I'll think about what you've said about preparing the way for a change, and perhaps you would be good enough to arrange a time with my secretary for us to meet tomorrow and discuss your eight considerations for implementing a change.'

'Yes I will' replied Tom rising to his feet. He collected his six guns up from the Chairman's desk and headed for the door with Max and me in invisible pursuit.

Part 7

'Tom didn't tell me any of this stuff Max, but I can see your point. I didn't make a good job of attempting to introduce the change that you showed me earlier. I made no preparation at all in terms of readying my people, I just arrived one morning and told them about it.'

'Exactly; can you see now that no matter how well you explained that change, you were up against invisible barriers; mental barriers?'

'Yes. I know how badly I can react to a change that is thrust upon me'.

'You mean like being made to wear a cowboy outfit without warning?'

Now Max laughed and after a pause so did I.

'Yes alright, so that's down to you Max.'

'It is?'

'Yes, if you had given me some warning, involved me in the deciding just what I was going to wear and helped me see how exciting the final result would be I might have been ready to accept the change you were introducing to me.'

We all laughed and I could see very well that Tom's explanation was effective. But we had more to learn from him, so Max and Ex spun me forward 24 hours where we found ourselves on the factory floor observing Tom and the Chairman once again.

Part 8

'**Introducing the change** needs as much care as planning it,' said Tom as the two of them walked slowly passed the large machine that had confronted Max and I when we first arrived. This time, however, the factory floor was busy with people going about their work.

'If you had asked the team here on the corrugator about the change whilst we were trying to make it work, they would all have been able to tell you what we were trying to achieve, what the plan was to make it happen, what the next step was to be and where it was expected to take us. People feel uncomfortable when they don't know what is going to happen next.'

'Yes I can see that,' replied the Chairman, 'and so you are saying that they will resist change simply because they don't know what's happening, irrespective of whether the change is a good idea or not?'

'Exactly you must **communicate the plan, the process and what is happening** if you want the support of the team.'

'But Tom, as the manager you can just tell them. They won't disobey you.'

'I beg to disagree,' said Tom. 'They probably won't appear to disobey, and may give the impression of trying, but in fact be resisting the change by simply letting things go wrong and not suggesting solutions when plans don't work. They are the ones who will have to make the change happen through their actions. But they can quietly lead it to failure, leaving us with the impression that it wasn't a good idea rather than that they didn't try to make it work. There is no way round this; to make change succeed we need the willing support of those we lead. Alongside this we must also **help people to let go** of their old way of doing things. We must honour the past not dismiss it. Take the people here.'

Now they had reached the end of the machine Tom had called the 'corrugator' and along the production line rolls of brown paper had been bonded and folded to make cardboard with a corrugated paper infill. At the end of the machine it was being cut into sheets and stacked on a pallet.

'Their method of cutting and stacking had to change as part of the big process change. We didn't just say 'here is a new way of doing things that will be much better'. This by implication to these people would have said 'the way you did this before wasn't good enough', and you can understand why that would cause resistance. We honoured the past by agreeing that the way we had done things so far had been effective and served us well, but that now we needed to move forward.

The third consideration here was to **minimise the difference** between the new and old way of doing things. People may resist because they feel self-conscious and awkward with something that is different, so we kept as many things the same as possible: the record sheet had a similar design although the content was different; we used the same colours to code the different weights and thicknesses of board. This all helps in the balance of things that are going to lead to positive or negative behaviour.'

Tom and the Chairman walked on, stepping aside as a forklift beeped at them and then passed carrying a stack of board into the area that they now approached. Here it was quieter and a variety of different machines were processing sheets of board into different shapes. They stopped to watch a cut and crease process where board was cut into the outline of a carton and then creased so that it would fold into the required shape.

'Here we had to give some **coaching in new skills**' said Tom. 'Some people may fear that they cannot do the new task, but they need to be given the appropriate skills and the opportunity to practise without being judged. Here they had a new process and a new piece of equipment and we gave them the opportunity to experiment with both. They gained confidence and so did not resist; in fact it had the opposite effect in that they gained some motivation at learning new skills. To help further with motivation we made sure people were **given recognition and support for extra work.** Change usually means more work for some people in the interim period where perhaps the old system is being replaced and things are running slowly at first or more mistakes than usual are being made. We discussed this in advance, identified the hot spots where we thought people may have more to do, and recognised them with simple and inexpensive incentives. People do not respond well to being taken for granted and the reverse is true in response to praise and reward.'

Now we moved to another part of this processing area to see a laminated printed paper being applied to sheets of board, these bright colours a contrast to the brown board that we had so far seen.

'I shouldn't give the impression that all of this was plain sailing. The team of supervisors had to keep their ears to the ground while we were introducing the changes. We had to **allow people to be heard.** We made sure that communication was two-way; we wanted to know what the views of the team were and particularly when something wasn't working as we had envisaged – we wanted to hear the problem and people's ideas for a solution. From the start we made it clear to everyone what the chain of responsibility was, whom they should talk to and that we wanted to hear their views. We constantly listened to feedback and reviewed it for changes we might need to make to the plan, or unexpected grievances that we might need to consider.

Tom and the Chairman finished their tour in the canteen where yesterday Tom had addressed the workforce in his cowboy outfit.

'There were two other things that were important' said Tom. One was to **anticipate the ripple effect.** Other things will be disrupted by the change, things that may look unrelated, but to the individuals concerned are important. A change in working hours may disrupt personal routines, or may affect things in other departments that weren't at first obvious. I made sure that the supervisors had good dialogue with their individual team members and we allowed a transition period to key the change to other activities. The last point I would make was the importance of me **clearly displaying my support through symbols and signals**. Management must send clear signals that they support the change either by actions or strong symbolic gestures. Some of the team members came up with the idea of promoting the change with these cowboy images. Tom pointed at the posters that we had noticed earlier. They illustrated three bullet holes, a cowboy with smoking six guns and the slogan 'let's shoot up those targets'. So I decided that since it was their idea they would support it and I would go along with it. That's why I have worn that Stetson hat around the factory for the last two weeks; it was a constant symbol of my commitment to the project and a reminder of what we were doing. You can imagine that it got lots of comment, especially when I accepted the challenge from the supervisors to wear a full cowboy outfit for the day if we succeeded. It worked, no one was in any doubt that I supported what was happening and was fully behind it. The posters were all part of the campaign to get people in the right frame of mind. By dealing positively with each of the eight elements that I have described to you around implementing the change, and because these were done against a background of good planning which had already minimised resistance, I believe we made our success.'

'I'm sure you did Tom,' replied the Chairman. 'I am really impressed with what you've told me and I can see that what you have achieved is not a piece of luck but the result of a well managed process. I would like you to come to the board meeting next week and present what you have done, I think we may have some opportunities for you.'

Tom was beaming as the Chairman left, and I wanted to congratulate him, but of course could not be seen or heard by my friend. Max and I sat together on Ex and I knew that we were once again about to leave.

'Is it time to go Max?'

'Yes. Did you learn from all of this?'

'Of course I did, you know that what you have shown me has been just what I needed to see. Goal Setting and Action Planning, Managing Performance, Reviewing Performance, and now Managing Change; no wonder I have been frustrated, no wonder my performance as a manager has been nothing better than average. You have shown me how some of my friends have used straightforward methods to get results, methods of which I had no knowledge. I feel really confident to go back and excel! But I have a request for you Max.'

'What is that?'

'A request and an apology.'

'Go on.'

'You surprised me when we met again after all these years and I know I didn't react too well. But now I've got used to what is happening and I don't really care how it's happening just that it is. But Max, could we do the cowboy thing one more time before we go?'

'Are you sure?'

'Yes, you were right about using my imagination, I guess I had stopped using it like I used to. But when I look at Tom who never did and saw how Janice could use her imagination to see possibilities, I reckon I've been missing out. Can we do just one more cowboy gallup as we go?'

'*Welcome back old buddy.*'

'Thanks Ex. Well Max?'

'I don't see why not. Never let go of the ability to use your imagination. If you can't imagine a different future you will never drive change, just be the subject of change.' And as Max lifted Ex's reins, I felt a shudder and, looking down, saw that our cowboy gear had been restored. Ex began to move and as he did music swelled. Max and I both shouted as Ex gathered pace plunging through a wall out into a car park and then into shimmering air as he gained greater speed, and the strings and brass boomed louder and louder. All cares had fallen from me and exhilaration took hold as we flew into bright, golden light and home?

Learning Questions

1. Why wasn't an enthusiastic and clear presentation enough to make the first planned change a success?
2. Why did Tom begin to 'sow the seeds' of an idea several weeks before he attempted to introduce the change?
3. How did Tom feel people might resist change if they were not managed correctly?
4. Why did Tom wear a cowboy hat around the factory floor?
5. How did Tom encourage his team members to use their imagination when introducing change?

Learning Summary – Managing Change

When introducing change a leader can reduce resistance by taking into account four important considerations at the planning stage:

*   Avoid surprises
*   Involve team members in planning the change
*   Make sure everyone shares the same vision of the outcome
*   Minimise the impact of past resentments

During introduction of the change there are a further eight issues that a leader should address in order to ensure that the change is accepted as positively as possible by team members. They are:

- communicate the plan, the process and what is happening
- help people to let go
- minimise the difference
- provide coaching in new skills
- give recognition and support for extra work
- allow people to be heard
- anticipate the ripple effect
- display support through symbols and signals

THE GHOST TRAINS (PERSONAL DEVELOPMENT)

Part 1

'It's home Max. But not as I know it.' The motorbike thrumming beneath us suggested the future and told me that we had not yet finished our journey.

'This is our final destination, soon you will have seen all you need to see,' replied Max.

I gazed around the same park where Max and I had re-united after my bungee jump. It was dusk, the light dimming and the temperature cool. Trees, grass, footpaths all seemed unchanged; but on the brow of a hill coloured lights and movement held my attention.

'You still up for some fun?' I noticed Max and I were not wearing helmets as he asked me this question. Instead of black leathers we wore blue jeans and t-shirts.

'Yes of course.' I felt an exciting lack of responsibility.

'All the fun of the fair?' Now I knew what those coloured lights and movement were. 'You bet. I love fairs.'

So Max and I roared up the hill anticipating exhilaration.

'When are we Max?'

'Twenty one years in your future,' Max was laughing as he told me this.

'I really don't think I want to see myself looking that old.'

'It's only 21 years, which will come round soon enough.'

'No it won't Max. Twenty one years is a long time; I've got a lot of living to do before I get here for real.' Discussion was cut short as we were engulfed by a flow of people: jostling, laughing, talking, shouting, people. We were washed by bright colourful lighting from stalls, rides, tents and caravans. Music from one place merging with and being replaced by something different from another, a sweet smell from a food stall, savoury from another. Groups chattering and laughing, some people looking wealthy and well dressed, others poor, others crass and tasteless; lovers, friends, families all merged into one compelling human soup. And through all this rode Max and I moving at speed with the unpleasant clammy feel of passing through people, actually going through a crowd was like being tickled with wet fish, it was not pleasant. 'Max stop it, please.'

'Nearly there,' he replied, and we emerged into a clear space beside a great wheel, brashly lit and static as people climbed aboard the gently swaying carriages.

I stood and stretched and then started as I saw a familiar face. It was Janice; despite the advance of years she was unmistakable.

'I've brought you here to think about outcomes,'

said Max, 'to see you how you and your friends turn out in your maturity. To see what you become!'

'Sounds serious'.

'It is,' he replied. 'I want you to focus your thinking on personal development and where it leads.'

'I don't I understand why we are in this place.' I said indicating the fair around us, 'Everywhere else you have taken me has been a workplace.'

'That's because this is about a bigger picture than work; personal development cannot be just about work. Our mind is the same mind in work and at home, we can't separate the two. When we develop a skill at work, that skill is with us in all areas of our life. That is true the other way around; skills and knowledge we gain in our personal lives may prove of value in our working lives. That's why I've brought you to see your friends in a non-working environment, to make sure we think about personal outcomes in the round, to consider what becomes of the whole person.'

Janice was holding the hand of a young girl, possibly 7 or 8 years old, who said 'When will Grandad be getting here, Grandma?'

'Hey,' still on the back of the bike my grip on Max's shoulder must have tightened.

'Sorry Max, but grandma! I can't believe this.'

'Grandad will be here soon,' said Janice.

'Why is he always late, Grandma?'

'Not always darling, but this is a busy time for him.'

'He's always busy, Grandma, and he's always late.'

Only children can get away with being this honest, I thought.

'We are nearly at the front of the queue,' persisted the little girl, ' if we miss it again it's another half hour and mum said you have to take me home for normal bed time, and that means we won't have time to go on it at all.'

Janice raised her hand in front of her face and appeared to talk at her palm.

'Darling where are you?'

'Hi this is Tom, please leave a message and I will get back to you as soon as I can,' replied her palm.

'Darling it's me, we are getting on the Flying Wheel, please meet us when we get back.'

They had reached the front of the queue. A short stocky figure approached and led them toward one of the swaying carriages.

That's when a familiar voice said, 'Not you two again.'

At first I didn't imagine that it was talking to Max and I, we were after all invisible to anyone here, but when it said 'Hey guys it's Mel stop ignoring me,' we both turned our eyes from Janice and her granddaughter and I guess my mouth fell open in surprise at the sight of Mel standing beside us. As the sights and sounds of the fair bubbled around us my grasp on reality appeared to be minimal.

'Mel?' For the moment my brain running out of anything but the obvious to say.

'Hi Max,' he smiled.

'Nice to see you again,' replied Max.

'Hey you two cool as you like, what on earth is going on here?'

'It's Mel,' said Max.

'I can see it's Mel,' I snapped, 'what is he doing here?'

'No need to talk about me as if I'm not here,' said Mel.

'No Mel sorry but why … how … what is going on?'

'I might ask you two the same question. I last saw you seven years ago, appearing out of nowhere as I breathed my last. That was a shock. Now here I am just going about my business seven years later and you pop up again, on a motorbike! I reckon it's you two that have some explaining to do.'

'Max?' I looked expectantly at him.

'Stopped being snappy now?' he replied, arms folded.

'Sorry Max, I'm just confused. Will you tell us both what's going on?'

'Well Mel can tell you why he is here and I will explain to Mel why we are here.'

'OK,' said Mel, 'I'm a consultant on the ghost train.' He pointed across the heads of the crowd to a large structure glowing in fluorescent blues and greens illustrated with cartoon images of skulls, coffins and hooded faces.

'But how, Mel? You died.'

'Yes I am dead. I'm a ghost.' Mel was talking slowly and as if to a child, 'That's why I'm a consultant on the ghost train. Wouldn't be much good if I was alive would it?'

'That's a big advance,' said Max, 'real ghosts on the ghost train'.

'Correct,' confirmed Mel. 'Once the scientists got to grips with all that stuff, what used to be called the paranormal just became … well, normal.'

'Real ghosts in the ghost train?' I repeated Max's words.

'Yes, the problem is they are not naturally scary, they're usually rather sad. My job is to get them to be spooky as per the expectations of the paying punter.'

'But you are dead Mel, why are you here at all?'

'Oh I see, your friend hasn't explained.'

'No I was hoping that you might,' said Max, 'in fact I was rather hoping that we could hang out with you for a short while whilst we catch up on your friends and make some sense of it all.'

'Mel, why are you here?' I repeated.

'I'm doing humanity service,' said Mel. 'Once the living got a grip on this 'life after death' thing it all became a lot more efficient. In the old days I believe that when you died you simply went to the holding room, had a quick review and film show of your best bits, got the thumbs up or thumbs down, and travelled on accordingly.'

Max nodded; I looked blank.

'Not any more. Now you arrive and your afterlife mentor refers to a hand-held computer and detailed report before conducting a performance appraisal during which certain key performance indicators are reviewed.'

'Key what?'

'Measures of how you have done. They don't simply want to know things like 'did you do good?' anymore, they want to know how much good did you do and how did it compare percentage wise with the bad, expressed as a numeric ratio. Mine was 4.4:1 so I was ok, but I fell down on the proportion of potential achieved. They're very tough on waste these days, and when my report went for assessment I wasn't passed fit to move on, well at least not to where I wanted to go anyhow. They offered me 10 years humanity service instead with a second performance appraisal at the end. I've had 7 years to learn what I missed and why. In fact

I've put in for early review, I might get away with only 8 years if I pass'.

'So you're a ghost because you didn't achieve your potential in life?'

'Yes, well not enough of it. If it falls below 33% you fail, or at least that was the measure when I died. Of course there's always someone lobbying to raise standards.'

'So since you're measured on doing good things I hope that means you will spend some time with us,' said Max.

'Of course I will; I see you were watching Janice.'

'Yes, I replied,' turning back toward the wheel, which had vanished.

Part 2

Max pointed upwards and we saw the missing wheel 100 feet above us, lit purple. As we watched, it tilted and flattened to a horizontal with the carriages hanging below. They encircled a compartment at the wheel's axis, the purple turned to orange. That central compartment held just one person who appeared to be working controls. In the carriages some people were animated pointing outwards no doubt at what they saw from their vantage points; I could see Janice and her granddaughter. Then the entire wheel began both to revolve and to travel away from us across the fair and out of our site.

'Here he comes,' said Mel pointing at a figure pushing through the crowd on the ground. 'Our old mate Tom. He's missed the ride. Isn't that the story of his life!'

'**That** Tom,' I exclaimed. 'So they got married.'

'Indeed they did and had two children,' replied Mel.

'He looks a lot older.'

'He's had a hard time these last few years, with Janice being made redundant and his job becoming so demanding.'

'Hasn't changed in one way though has he Mel? He never could get anywhere on time. But I'm surprised by what you are telling me, these two were the bright young things, they were successful when they were young; Janice at the Rodeo theatre and Tom managing change at the packaging company, I always imagined they had star-studded careers ahead of them.'

'So did they. They burned bright when they were young, and both lost their way a bit in later life. That's one of the things I have been here to observe,' said Mel 'to understand how potential is achieved or missed.'

'Are they unhappy, Mel?' I asked.

'I would say disappointed rather than unhappy.' replied Mel 'They've both done ok in their careers but life has been a series of disappointments for them both, and now Tom is having to work hard to keep them afloat. They don't have the options or the lifestyle that either had hoped for.'

'Have you worked out why, Mel?'

'Yes I think so. Neither of them ever took their own development seriously. Consider your comment about Tom always being late; we both remember him as disorganised; he was loveable and often inspired, but unreliable. That was something he never got on top of, his personal organisation and time management is terrible, so he is always at a disadvantage. His development happened sporadically and by accident;

he would get some good advice from someone, or stumble across a good training session and pick up something of value. He believed that he never had time to do more and, of course, his own disorganisation meant that this was always true.'

'He has a really good understanding of managing change.'

'Exactly that became his thing, he could teach others about it and do it well himself. But he left his development incomplete, never understood that there was much more to be learned, without which he could only ever be partially effective. He never saw the big picture, never planned his own development so never made it happen. His ability to achieve the things he wanted in life, either at work or in his private life, have as a result always been limited. And you can say the same of Janice.'

'Success and satisfaction are not just about work, Mel. Perhaps they chose a different kind of success, put their private lives first.'

'No, it doesn't work that way. The skills and knowledge you must develop to succeed with work are in many cases the same as those you need to succeed in the other areas of your life. They have both been as frustrated in their private lives as in their working lives.'

'We saw Janice turn that theatre from failure to success, so why didn't she make such a great success of herself?'

'She did have success; she did well, made her mark. A lot of people would be proud to achieve what she achieved. But she could have done so much better, done what she wanted to do on her own terms. You saw the pleasure, satisfaction, self-esteem she gained from her early success; but nothing is more effective at undermining those positive feelings than the frustration of underperformance. That's what happened to her. She was great at Goal Setting and Action Planning in terms of the business, but completely failed to do it in terms of herself. She never mastered a range of other skills that were easily within her ability because she didn't even know of their existence. She assumed that because she had started so well it would keep going. If only she had planned her development and worked at it, developed a full suite of leadership skills, she would have had so much more success. She would have had more choices of job and type of work and the constant satisfaction of achievement and reward. As it is, she did ok; just ok.

They both wanted to retire early, Janice expecting to work for another few years before they did so and Tom hoping that he would get further promotion to boost his income in his last working years. Now those hopes are gone and they are both under pressure with Tom working harder than ever. Tom is creative and wants to follow his heart and play music; he hoped that in early retirement he could do this. Janice loves amateur theatre; she does a little but looks back now and sees that she could have done so much more. She thinks that life is just like that and you can't do everything you want, but the shame of it is that if she had developed herself more effectively she would have found the opportunity to do many of the things that she hoped for when she was younger. So many opportunities have passed by them both and they have ended up where they didn't want to be, under financial pressure in their later years and looking to work harder, rather than easing out of work into a stress free retirement.'

'What about you Mel? Are you ok now?' I asked.

'Oh yes. I have learned so much over the past years, watching people make more or less of themselves, recognising where I failed. Once I left school I breathed a sigh of relief and thought 'thank goodness that lot is over with, now I can get on with living and forget about learning.' I was completely wrong and paid the price. I had no idea that I should see school as just the beginning and plan for my development in later life. I learned things when I took new jobs and thought that was enough, it wasn't. I expected my employers to take care of my training, and hated it when they did. I never enjoyed the interruption to my job to go on training courses. And so I never approached learning after school seriously. I ended up as a manager having completely underestimated the role. I know now that I could have been very good.I think back to the way I tried to lead people and cringe with embarrassment at my ignorance and stupidity. I can see just why I didn't get respect from the people I managed and without their respect, co-operation and support I became increasingly stressed. Couple that with not looking after myself physically and you could see my illness coming. I got nowhere near my potential, I wasted my life.'

'Blimey Mel, you must be feeling pretty bad about all that.'

'Not any more, I'm pleased to have had the chance to see what happened. I can help you if you want.'

'That would be great, what can you tell me?'

'Why don't we go and take a look at the other two of our gang of five?'

'Flo?'

'And you.'

'Do I really want to see myself at 58, Mel?'

'We're not going to give you a choice, are we Max?'

'No. It's our last visit before I take you back where you belong, we're going to make the most of it.' Max grinned and revved the bike.

'We can see you and Flo together, I know just the spot. Max, can you oblige?'

'Of course, I'll take you both.'

Just then we were bathed in pink light as the wheel reappeared above us. Tom was waving. The short stocky figure that had shown Janice to the wheel

re-appeared, but with two others who looked exactly the same in shape. The three of them moved to the area where the wheel would be landing and then one of their heads swivelled 180 degrees on its shoulders to talk with one of the others. I must have let out a gasp because Mel said 'I was surprised the first time I saw one of those. They're MP's, mechanical people. These days they get used for everything humans can't be bothered to do.'

'Come on, Max,' I said, 'enough surprises. Let's get going.' We were on our way to meet my destiny.

Part 3

I think I fell asleep wedged between Mel and Max on the back of that bike (an imaginary friend and a ghost!), and no wonder I did. My mind was exhausted with all that had happened. That bungee jump was frightening, meeting Max was extraordinary. To journey back in time and see a younger me, to see Janice transforming the theatre and using goal setting and action planning so well; forward in time to see Mel breath his last and me in charge of selling those odd vehicles and an expert in performance management; back but still forward to see Flo on that great ship and her methods for developing performance; back again to see a fresh-faced me getting managing change all wrong and a bright young Tom getting it all right. And now I find myself in a funfair of my distant future seeing my friends all over again in their later life. It has been incredible, fascinating and exhausting. But Max had said he had one more place to take me.

He rode us through time and space to what I later learned was the following morning and less than a mile from the funfair where we had seen Janice and Tom. I woke with a lurch to find Mel standing next to the bike and elevator doors opening in front of us. A motorbike in a lift may not be too unusual but when the doors opened onto a graveyard, well!

Part 4

'Surprise,' said Mel.

There were gravestones in neat rows, each at the head of a tidily kept raised grass covered oblong. At the four corners of this space where a planting of colourful shrubs and what looked like a vending machine by a bench. Above us was a flat roof painted white and ahead, after about the tenth row of stones, was a parapet, beyond that a skyline of rooftops.

'I guess you've never seen a multi storey grave yard before,' said Mel. 'When land became scarce this idea took off. There's a 10 foot depth of soil on each floor and in this building there are six floors. It's not soil as you would know it; it's a semi-synthetic soil containing fast breakdown enzymes that absorb any liquids and gases effectively. It's popular and if you would like to follow those people I will show you my plot.' Mel had pointed at two figures who had left a second lift and were 20 metres ahead of us. It was Flo and me, Flo carrying a bunch of flowers. As we caught up with them we heard a voice from somewhere to our left.

'Aha. Rich Eric. I knew him well.' The voice was strangely pleasant; rounded and melodic.

Flo and the aging me (actually I was quite impressed, I looked to be in pretty good shape) stopped and looked. We all peered into an open grave that was being prepared by the owner of the voice.

'Oh I do apologise,' said this person who we now saw standing in the grave holding a shovel in one hand and a skull in another. It appeared that he had been talking to the skull.

'This soil doesn't hold things like real earth does. This,' lifting the skull, 'has crept from the next plot,' he pointed to his right. I looked at the stone and read *Eric Harley, edited from life but not from memory*. 'He commissioned me,' said the speaker as he stepped out of the grave by elongating his legs until his torso was above ground level, stepping out and then shrinking his legs to return to the broad short stature of an MP.

'Eric was the editor of the local paper, now it looks like he's lost his headline. Ha ha.'

'I didn't know MPs had a sense of humour' said Flo.

'A humour chip was an optional extra with early MPs. Eric loved a good laugh. Who are you here to visit?'

'Mel Gibbon' we both replied.

'Ah yes, dear Mel. Fifteen ahead then two rows to the right, I'm sure he hasn't moved!' and then as if a secondary programme had kicked in inside the MP 'Oh I do beg your pardon, inappropriate humour, that is a problem with this chip.'

At that moment a small group of mourners passed on their way to the lift. All dressed in black they included a fashionably dressed mature lady arm in arm with a much younger man, her heels clicked on the concrete floor. 'Come along Marlon,' she said to her companion 'let's go and celebrate outrageously.' The look in her eye suggested he was not her son.

'Haven't we seen her before, Max?'

'Yes she does seem familiar'.

Flo and I were now headed in the direction indicated. We followed.

'Goodbye,' said the MP with the pleasant voice, descending again to his work, 'enjoy your visit and I must put Eric back to bed, before he's missed. Haha! Oh sorry – damn'.

Arriving at Mel's grave Flo put the flowers into a stone vase that formed part of the headstone and then the two of them, that is Flo and me (I hope you are paying attention? That's me as in me over there 21 years older than I actually am when writing this, not me as in me here watching me over there. Ok?), stood at the foot of the grave. The older me took a hip flask from their coat pocket and gave some of the content to Flo. They both drank in turn raising the cup and saying 'In memory of Mel.'

'What it is to have friends,' said Mel, although of course they couldn't hear him.

'It's nice to do this once a year,' said Flo, ' pity we can't get Janice and Tom along, then we could all go for a meal together afterwards. Ever see them?'

'No,' replied the older me, 'not for years. I tried to stay in touch but you know what Tom was like, so disorganised.'

'Shame,' said Flo. 'I lost touch with them when I went to sea.'

'The two stood for a few moments gazing at Mel's stone.

'I think I'm going to cry,' said Mel.

That's when I had my idea.

'Max come and stand here' I said, moving to stand by Mel's stone.

'What?'

'Come and stand behind Mel's stone, quick.'

'Why?'

'Come on Max, just do it'

'Ok' and Max moved to stand behind me.

'No not behind me Max, here beside me so you are standing directly behind the stone.'

'Are you feeling alright?' asked Max, 'perhaps we've overdone it a bit with the travelling.'

'Quiet,' I hissed. Flo had begun to talk again. Looking at her closely I noticed that she was gracefully ageing, inevitable I suppose, and I had to admit some pleasure in observing how well I looked!

'Something I meant to ask you,' said Flo still gazing wistfully at Mel's stone and sipping at the drink. 'You have managed to make a real success of yourself. You look great and you have such a good lifestyle, yet when we were all younger I never would have guessed that of the five of us you would be the one who did so well. How did you do it?'

'I just knew you were going to ask me that,' the older me replied, and looking straight over the top of the gravestone and smiling into Max's eyes, added 'Didn't I, Max?'

Max gasped. 'Yes you did,' replied Flo, 'I am curious to know how you did it.'

The older me winked at Max and said 'the answer is over there,' nodding toward the stone and still looking at Max, 'isn't it?'

'He can't see me,' said Max clearly confused, his face displaying concern as he turned to me and then seeing the smug look on my face, he turned back to the older me and Flo.

'You mean Mel,' said Flo 'he was your secret?'

'He gave me a serious lesson in what can happen if you get it badly wrong,' replied the older me.

'I get it,' said Max, 'very clever, you can't really see me at all.'

'You can't have just changed yourself so radically though.' said Flo.

'Oh yes I can, Max.' The older me was still looking at Max.

Max gasped again.

'What do you mean you can, Max?' asked Flo.

'So can you,' said the older me. 'Anyone can Max. Anyone can make the best of themselves if they apply themselves to the task.'

Max turned to me. 'This is just a memory trick isn't it?'

'Yes but it's a good one isn't it? Had you going.'

'You will remember this, and that's why you put me in that exact position.'

'Yes I will remember to look above Mel's headstone

and say those words in 21 years time just to give you a shock. Impressed?'

'Yes very, but let's pay attention, this is the bit we are supposed to be listening to.' Max turned again to the older me and Flo.

Part 6

'Come on. Stop being so enigmatic and tell me what you did.' This was more of an instruction from Flo than a request. The older me complied.

'I learned a big lesson in my mid 30's Flo. I realised that I'd been drifting in terms of maximising my own potential.'

'How did you realise?'

'A few friends helped me, Flo,' another smile to Max.

'Stop it,' said Max.

'The big lesson for me was that it is **my responsibility to plan and make my own development happen**. I can't expect others to do it; you know, wait for some employer to send me on a course, or rely on school teachers to push me along. It was down to me. And once I realised that, I began to take it seriously. I had first to ask **'what do I want to achieve with my life?'** and then **'what skills do I need to develop to achieve it?'** In answer to the first I knew that I would like to be successful enough in my working life to live comfortably and successfully in my family and social life. To be able to support my family and have choices throughout my life, rather than be trapped in one place or direction by lack of skill or resource. I was

Goal Setting in personal **and** business terms. Having decided what I wanted to achieve I then had to consider what skills I needed to develop. I learned that there were three areas to consider **performance, body and mind**.

Performance required me to become expert in the business I had chosen to work in, to know the detail of my job: the product, the organisation, the competition, the market place, the processes we used. What was needed was obvious until it came to leading people, then I found a whole range of unexpected skills, but I will come back to that.

Body was about physical well being. Poor diet and minimal exercise mean the mind will slow along with the body, making illness more likely with the associated disruption to life and mental well being. Whilst I have never been a fitness fanatic I made a point of looking after myself, getting some exercise, eating a healthy diet and avoiding damaging excess.

Mind was an unexpected challenge, a key to unlocking everything else. I had to get my thoughts in order, build my self-esteem, unlock my imagination in order to become resourceful, control my emotions rather than letting them control me. These things brought with them the confidence necessary to succeed.'

'I've never thought about my development in this way,' said Flo, 'please dig deeper for me. I understand that you kept yourself in good shape and took the time to learn about your business, but what about the unexpected skills you mention; and building self-esteem sounds more easily said than done.'

'I worked at learning more, Flo, I read carefully about leadership and what was required. I took a long hard look at some successful leaders around me, watching what they did and how they conducted themselves. I recognised a set of skills that it seemed clear I would have to develop if I was to succeed. Then I made a plan for my own development and over several years I made a point of mastering each skill on my list. I made a plan, carried it out and found my ability and confidence grew; along with that came the success I had set as my goal. I took responsibility and made it happen. What I really learned on that journey was that I had the ability but had never believed it. I learned how to Max.'

'I never did,' said Flo, 'learn to Max that is. There are some things that I am good at, but I don't have the confidence or all round ability to do as well as you.'

'So you think, Flo, but you will be the one holding yourself back. What have you done about your development?'

'I hate training courses if that's what you mean.'

'Well that's your choice, but is that because you saw them just as a disruption to your work rather than an opportunity to develop yourself?'

'I have never considered my personal development, I just don't like training.'

'So how have you replaced that? What alternatives did you choose, what did you arrange for yourself instead of training courses?'

'Nothing. I see your point, but it's too late now.'

'It's never too late to build your life skills, Flo, and it won't take as long as you think.'

'Ok so what about this list of skills you decided you needed?'

'Let's go and sit down, it's a bit morbid stood here looking at Mel's stone.'

'Hey,' said Mel, 'nothing morbid about me,' which of course they didn't hear.

'You're right. Goodbye Mel,' said Flo to the stone and then turned toward a bench amongst some shrubs a few metres away.

'Bye Mel,' said the older me, looking again at Max and winking before following Flo.

'Coffee?' asked Flo stopping at a vending machine to the side of the seating area. Passing one steaming cup to the older me and keeping one for herself she sat on the bench, pressing the mute button in the arm rest to turn off the Mozart piano concerto playing softly from the shrubs. 'Come on then,' she said 'tell me the rest.'

'I made a list, Flo, a list that fitted what I wanted to achieve.'

'And what was that?'

'I wanted to become an effective manager and leader. I divided my list into five parts.

The first was my Personal Development. I accepted responsibility for my own development, made an **assessment of my strengths and weaknesses** against the list of skills I thought I needed and made **plans to put right my weaknesses**. I also recognised that **personal networking** was important and would become increasingly so in later life. I made a point of meeting people and building a network of good business friends. Finally I dealt with my own **confidence and self-esteem**; I learned valuable thinking disciplines and methods without which I would never have been able to do all that I have.

The second part of my list was Giving Direction and Getting Results. This included the ability to use **goals and action plans**, to **solve problems** and make more good **decisions** than bad, to **lead the culture** of a group of people, to **manage performance** and **projects**, and all of this needed what I came to know as the **Hidden Treasure** skills, those skills that a leader needs in order to get others to follow willingly and invest their initiative and effort in the group's enterprise.

The third part was to lead Innovation and Manage Change. Change is constant, achieving and maintaining advantage over competing groups requires innovation, which of course needs change.

The fourth was to manage Resources effectively. Physical, financial and human resources must all be maximised if you want to maximise your chance of success, and alongside this must be a willingness and ability to understand and exploit **new technologies**.

And the fifth was to Select, Recruit and Develop the right people.

That's it in summary, and I set out to sharpen my ability in all of those things without exception.'

'That sounds like a big job, but I see the sense in what you are saying.'

'It was an undertaking of years, and once I had the basics under my belt, it never stopped and never has.'

'How did you learn?'

'Some things I picked up from observing others doing things well. I had one boss in particular who was a great example and I learned so much from simply watching him. I kept an eye out for training courses that could help me fill a gap in my development plan; in some cases I bought and studied books or other learning media.'

'I can see all of that; I just wish I had seen it before

now. My list would have been different to yours.'

'What would you have done Flo?'

'I always wanted to work with children. I got into the work that I do by chance; my father wanted me to get a 'proper job' and helped me early on. Then things just developed by chance. I've done well I suppose, but I do look back with some regret that I couldn't do what I think would have really fulfilled me.'

'And what now Flo, what are you plans looking ahead?'

'Frankly I'm looking ahead to retirement in a couple of years.'

'And what will you do?'

'I have a few ideas?'

'Plans?'

'Not yet.'

'You could use this same thinking to make your retirement more rewarding than your working life. The idea of developing to succeed should not just be about our working lives.'

'I'll think about that,' said Flo, 'anyway shall we go and eat now we've said hello to Mel for another year?'

'Great idea I'm famished,' replied the older me, and the pair headed back to the elevator by which they had arrived.

'Time for us to go as well,' said Max.

'That's it off you go and leave me in this depressing place,' answered Mel.

'Want a lift somewhere?' asked Max.

'Back to the fair for me,' said Mel ' but I think I'd rather float thank you, that bike of yours made me feel distinctly unwell.'

We made our goodbyes to Mel, and Max pointed

the bike to the edge of barrier where the light skyline had been replaced by a shimmering light. 'Time to go home at last' said Max. 'You ready?'

'Dem bones, dem bones, dem dry bones – haha!' sung in a rounded and melodic voice was the last thing I heard as we shot forward toward the end of my adventure.

Learning Questions

1. Why did Max choose not to visit a working environment for this last destination?
2. What is the common and significant element of Tom and Janice's experience in this chapter?
3. What advice did Mel give about responsibility?

Learning Summary – Personal Development

We must take responsibility for our own development by setting clear personal goals and planning how we will build the skills required to achieve those goals.

To become an effective manager/leader **a valuable set of skills is**:

1. Personal Development
   - discover what skills and qualities are needed to achieve your goals,
   - assess your own skills honestly against them and plan how to build those skills that are weaknesses
   - consider performance, body and mind
   - build personal networks with others
   - think of confidence and self esteem as legitimate and neccesary objectives for development

2. Giving Direction and Getting Results
   - goal setting and action planning
   - problem solving and decision making

- leading culture
- managing performance
- developing people
- assertive communication
- leadership
- coaching
- delegation
- team building

3. Leading Innovation and Managing Change

4. Managing Resources effectively
   - financial understanding
   - managing physical resources

5. Selection, Recruitment and Development of people

37

ARE YOU READY?

'Max.'

How gracefully Ex had galloped on that final short journey to the car park. Max waved a cheery goodbye as if he would see me tomorrow and I recalled he had done the same all those years ago. How simply the two had vanished, silently disappearing as I waved back.

'Max!'

How disorientated I had felt driving those few miles to the 'Black Horse' where we were all to meet, and realising on arrival that for my friends only a short time had passed since we separated after the bungee jump.

'Maxine!' the insistent voice belonged to Flo.

'Sorry,' I replied.

'You were miles away,' said Janice.

'On planet Maxine,' added Tom 'and I thought your imagination had retired years ago.'

'That bungee jump really shook you up,' this was Mel, 'and you're the last person I thought would have a problem with it, our resident tomboy and all that.'

'No I'm fine,' I replied, ' I just got a surprise that's all'; thinking *yes I was always the tomboy, the wild courageous cowgirl in my childhood mind to the one who organised the damn bungee for today. Give me a challenge and I was up for it, always!* And that's when I realised that this was just one more challenge that I must take up, to learn the lessons I had been presented with and pass them on to my friends. After all, that was no different to what I should do as a good leader by developing the skills of my work team.

We turned our heads when raised voices cut through the buzz of conversation. A man swayed to his feet, 'that's outrageous' were the only words I could discern as he shouted at the woman who was with him, pushing her through the crowd toward the door. She looked meek and sad. He staggered past leering suggestively at Janice in a way that caused Tom to bristle; then they were gone. 'He was a nasty piece of work,' said Mel, and I agreed, but then found a smile and an accompanying swell of good humour as puzzle pieces slid into place inside my head. Of course I had seen her before at every stage of my journey with Max. But that wasn't the only puzzle to be solved. Max had helped me understand my own development which called for pieces to be put in place, some of which I hadn't known even existed, pieces that would now sit quietly in the background behind my success.

All can change, that was Max's lesson even though the course may not at first be obvious. Effort is needed and important ideas must be painstakingly fitted together, our futures are not defined. Perhaps there exists a rough draft of our life story, ready for us to edit if we will only take responsibility. I could help them learn what I had learned. I could show them how to build better futures than those I had foreseen for them, I could point them in the right direction to be the successes they wanted to be and achieve their true potential. Doesn't mean they'll do it, I mused, but hey!

Mel was tucking into a plate of chips when I laid my hand on his arm. This was going to be a challenge, I breathed in hard, stepped onto the edge that was the beginning of my chance to help my friends, and jumped.

'You first Mel.'

'What?'

'Are you ready to Max?'

The End (ish)

SOME PRINCIPLES

What follows are the assumptions and guiding principles that lie behind the story of Max.

- All human beings have substantial potential.

- Most human beings have a tendency to underestimate their own potential and the potential of others.

- All can develop themselves toward their potential, but only if they recognise their responsibility for this and apply themselves persistently to do so.

- Groups of people working together as a team can achieve to a level that is significantly beyond what those people would achieve acting as individuals.

- Leaders can create teams if those leaders employ the correct skills and strategies.

- Leaders must recognise the importance of the development of their team members and create an environment where this happens.

- Any group of people can work together as a team.

The most effective teams will be those where the member's natural talents and attitudes complement each other.

* A leader can lead a team to excel by intelligent use of Goals and Plans of Action. These can be achieved when Performance is ensured by proactive leadership.

* Change is a constant and should be used to maintain advantage and motivation.

The Author and The Blue Water Partnership

Gordon Roscoe is a Senior Partner in The Blue Water Partnership. Gordon graduated with a degree in Law in 1976, and joined the Bowater Corporation as a General Management trainee, commencing his working life in the Paper and Packaging industry. His career has taken him into the Automotive Industry, the Music Industry and latterly the 'People Development' Industry.

Gordon developed an early interest in motivation at work as a young manager puzzling over the varied performances of team members. Experience around the world showed that people management challenges are universal, only the local detail changes but never the underlying issues of motivation, influence and leadership.

With much management experience under his belt, Gordon entered the world of training and development in 1992. As Operations Director for a training organisation he observed the successes and failures of various training initiatives and linked them to the shortcomings of traditional approaches to developing managers. In particular the common failure of management theory and training seminars to help managers make meaningful changes in their workplace.

His conclusion is that the average manager gets only a small part of the average person's potential at work. This is a failure of leadership; yet with some subtle changes in style and approach, managers can unlock abilities and attitudes that drive teams and organisations to success. The Blue Water Partnership was formed in 2000 to present alternative solutions to the challenge of helping managers develop leadership skills. Blue Water is a steadily growing organisation with a network of experienced implementing partners throughout the UK and Europe, and a clutch of clients who are happy to confirm the impressive success that they have enjoyed as a result.

www.thebluewater.com

Also by this author

Hidden Treasure

Novel, Textbook or novel textbook?

Many leaders despair because they can't find people of the right ability. The chances are that they already have them, but they don't know how to unlock their potential. That is the Hidden Treasure of the title.

The demolition of an old factory building is the unexpected trigger that unlocks the reader's journey around a set of people and circumstances whose stories overlap and whose destinies share a single strand.

The story slides backward and forward in time and a picture emerges which powerfully illustrates the outcomes of leadership behaviours. It shows their impact on organisations of all kinds and on the wider society that surrounds them. This unpredictable trip takes in a factory, a school, a newspaper, a neighbourhood regeneration scheme and a world-class sporting club. It tumbles the reader into a sports stadium filled with 40,000 screaming spectators, a school playground where the stars are arguably a ferret and a purple fountain and the unexpected thoughts of a blind and crippled elderly lady. It explains the story behind the newspaper headline A MARTIAN ATE MY GRANNY and the mystery of who bugged the conference room is revealed.

This is an antidote to textbooks and a manager's invaluable accomplice. It is a development text but for the widest possible audience. The book shows how voluntary organisations, commercial businesses and public sector institutions all must depend on the same core set of skills if they are to prosper, i.e. the skills of their leaders and people managers to be able to move others to perform to the best of their ability.

The author's optimism about human capability is based on observed experience as a developer of people managers. The concept proposed by this book is that people can achieve their best potential when gathered together in a supportive team and that only the leader can make this happen.

Hidden Treasure sets out to take the reader on a learning journey to understand the skills and confidence required to build and lead teams. The author asserts that many exceptional leaders are simply ordinary people behaving exceptionally, and what makes them exceptional is their ability to get ordinary people to behave exceptionally!